"Nikki Stern wields her enviable wit to tilt at society's windmills in a voice empowered by her starring role in arguably the most seminal event of our lifetimes. The painful and public loss of her husband on September 11 and the changes to her life since that day mirror the patterns of loss, anger, despair and rebuilding that our nation as a whole continues to experience. Before you know it, you'll feel a sense of optimism born of the notion that if she can greet each day with humor, intelligence and yes, hope – then it seems possible that we may all collectively as a nation be able to do so as well."

    Christal Smith, producer
    Contributor, *The Huffington Post*

"Through no fault of her own, Nikki Stern was catapulted into the ranks of America's moral authorities. She had the unique good sense to question why this should be so, or why we need such authorities in the first place. Her book is cogent, tough-minded and revelatory."

    Peter Trachtenberg, author, *The Book of Calamities*
    Winner, 2009 Phi Beta Kappa Ralph Waldo Emerson Award

"Nikki is a true daughter of the Enlightenment: skeptical of authority and absolutes; reliant on the goodness of people; confident in the power of critical thinking; hopeful for the future. Hers is a rare, bright, courageous and yes, humorous voice, especially when she subjects media and celebrity culture to a hilarious mental frisking. Yet she is open to dialogue with those who disagree with her, and humble enough to know she does not have all the answers."

    the Rev. Dr. John D. Sweet, pastor
    Presbyterian Church (U.S.A.)

Because I Say So

THE DANGEROUS APPEAL
OF MORAL AUTHORITY

NIKKI STERN

Bascom Hill Books
Minneapolis

BASCOM HILL
PUBLISHING GROUP

Bascom Hill Publishing Group
212 3rd Avenue North, Suite 290
Minneapolis, MN 55401
612.455.2293
www.bascomhillpublishing.com

ISBN: 978-1-935456-08-7
ISBN: 1-935456-08-3
LCCN: 2009913757

Cover design by Alan Pranke

Printed in the United States of America

*This book is dedicated to a critical thinker and a positive thinker –
my father and mother.*

TABLE OF CONTENTS

INTRODUCTION

On September 11, 2001, Jim Potorti, my husband of eleven years, was killed where he worked at the World Trade Center. The next day, I had a new identity as a "9/11 widow." I also apparently had something else: moral authority.

The moral authority assumed to belong to the victims' relatives was never clearly defined, but we seemed to gain special status. As far as I could tell, being a 9/11 family member made us, in the view of some, not just more sympathetic but also more virtuous. Granted, we had become a public symbol for the country's collective grief, a difficult position for anyone to pull off while trying to mourn privately, search for remains, and wait for questions to be answered. But what I honestly couldn't accept was that we 9/11 families had, by virtue of our terrible experience, acquired any sort of grief-related moral wisdom.

Americans don't think much about moral authority; they accept it without considering what it means. We may be inclined to question or protest other kinds of authority (at least if we're paying attention) but something about the notion of moral authority prompts a different reaction. Moral authority is, we believe, about what is wise and decent and brave and, well, moral. In its ideal form, such authority belongs to and is exercised by people or institutions that exhibit all those qualities. Yes, the wrong people may have claimed and continue to claim moral authority; but we don't question the viability of the concept itself. The idea of a special authority is appealing, which may be why we appear determined to find and invest our hopes and dreams in someone or some group of someones whose qualities we think set them apart from the rest of us: designated heroes or heroic entities of elevated moral character who we trust to know the right thing to do in any given situation.

Don't get me wrong; I firmly believe in virtues such as wisdom, decency, and courage. I hope people we put in positions of authority or people we look to for advice or leadership will have some of those qualities. But moral authority itself isn't a virtue and, if we think it is, we've failed to understand its limitations.

Moral authority is often less about being moral and more about being right, gaining power by standing apart and above. The moral nature of the authority discourages questions. Remember the argument our parents used when they wanted us to do something: "Because I say so"? That's moral authority's end game. In matters that deserve or perhaps even require discussion – how to build a 9/11 memorial, rebuild Lower Manhattan, authorize war, arrest dissidents, condone torture, treat our elderly, teach our children, or even engage in humanitarian acts around the world – moral authority is the guy who makes a declaration, sits back, folds his arms, and closes his mind.

Because decisions or declarations made under the guise of moral authority don't need to be justified, moral authority feels static, unchanging. The world of moral authority is circular and insular. What we understand to be true becomes righteous, and is righteous because it's true. We don't doubt or argue with those we believe are operating from high moral ground because, well, they're on high moral ground. And so it goes.

My unhappiness with moral authority's continued presence in our culture is partly a function of how it's used and by whom. An assortment of victims, spiritual advisors, talking heads, celebrities, bloggers, and others has vied for the privilege of being seen as having a special kind of insight or knowledge. We know they don't all deserve moral authority. We could become more selective about assigning moral authority and in monitoring how it's used. We could make sure it's reserved for those who we decide are appropriately wise, compassionate, and moral.

But that's not good enough; it leaves moral authority standing as an *ideal*. We have to question moral authority's fitness to serve as the basis for making political, legal, medical, or even moral determinations. Moral authority is about power – the power to persuade, to influence, and sometimes to force. Such an authority stands above, answers to no one, and relies on *being right* more than on *doing what's right*.

Moral authority shouldn't be viewed as a worthy touchstone. It doesn't belong as part of American cultural thought. Moral authority doesn't solve problems but rather creates them, often injecting inflexibility into a process better served by consensus. I'm not arguing against the idea of moral standards or in favor of detached cynicism; we should never stop aspiring to what is right and good. But moral authority isn't how we get there.

This book is part memoir, part cultural critique, and part invitation to dialogue. The world seems at times filled with people convinced beyond the shadow of a doubt they are uniquely qualified to know and represent what is right. I'm not one of them, which leaves me alternately amused and amazed that I put my foot down – or stuck my neck out (choose your body part) – on the subject of moral authority. Maybe writing about the shortcomings of a longstanding philosophical and cultural concept takes some nerve, but it doesn't require moral authority.

Chapter One

BECAUSE I SAY SO

"We think so because other people all think so; or because – or because
– after all we do think so; or because we were told so, and think we must
think so; or because we once thought so, and think we still think so; or
because, having thought so, we think we will think so..."

Henry Sidgwick—English Victorian philosopher, circa 1850

Two weeks after 9/11, my husband's company, Marsh McLen-
nan, held a service at St. Patrick's Cathedral in New York for
the 290 employees who died in the attacks. I sat by myself as close
to the front as possible. The featured speaker was Rudy Giuliani,
whose performance during his tenure as New York's mayor left
many of us unimpressed, to say the least. That day, however, he
was mesmerizing, in large part because his anguish was so honest,
and his feelings so clearly a reflection of the audience's own. A
video of the services shows me in all my raw emotion, hanging
over the edge of the pew into the aisle; such was the effect of the
mayor's words as well as his absolutely pitch-perfect delivery.
Honestly, I'm not sure I remember what he said; I knew only that
he was a kindred spirit who understood how I felt. He got it. Never

mind that he'd already given a similar speech hundreds of times at other memorial services and funerals during this terrible period and would do so a hundred times more. He tapped into our pain and allowed his own to show. He knew it and we knew it.

As I left the service, I overheard a woman say to her companion, "The mayor certainly speaks from a position of moral authority." I looked around in surprise. Immediately after the attacks, Giuliani's combination of leadership and compassion had earned him the sobriquet "America's mayor" in the local and national press. His empathy and eloquence had touched us all that day. Giuliani also had a reputation for being stubborn, self-righteous, and frequently tone-deaf when it came to his constituents. Perhaps he had changed, but had he also acquired moral authority? I didn't see how.

The notion was getting a lot of play after 9/11, whether in regard to the moral authority assigned to the families or assumed by the administration responding to the attacks. I wanted to know what people meant (or thought they meant) by those words, so I began looking for a clear definition. I've been looking ever since.

The phrase "moral authority" is in the titles of dozens of books and hundreds of articles about subjects as diverse as education, medicine, the penal system, business, and foreign policy. I've also found references online, from a site on effective salesmanship to one advocating white supremacy. There's a link to an article by a professor of law at Southwest University who's given some thought to the subject and another link to a blogger from Chicago who appears to have given next to none.

Wiktionary, the online dictionary, has an unattributed definition that dates from the mid-nineteenth century: "Moral authority (of a person, institution, or written work) [is] the quality or characteristic of being respected for having good character or knowledge, especially as a source of guidance or an exemplar of proper conduct."[1] The definition, although old-fashioned, squares with how our culture views moral authority as a passive set of admirable qualities. Eventually, anyone who has that authority uses it.

Since the word authority seems to change the status of moral (the inverse is also true; authority is made acceptable and even welcome because of the word moral), I've looked at each of them separately. *Merriam-Webster* defines authority principally as the "power to influence or command thought, opinion, or behavior" (the secondary meaning of expertise is also included).[2] Moral is defined as being: "of or relating to principles of right and wrong in behavior."[3] Combining those two definitions appears to produce a moral authority that gives its owner the power to influence thought, opinion, or behavior in matters of right or wrong. That's a lot of power, the kind we seem less disposed to question. It's as if someone says, "Ah, *moral* authority, well, that's different."

In this instance, we're not talking about the kind of authority that implies knowledge or training. The woman at the memorial service was not suggesting Rudy Giuliani was an expert on the subject of ethics. His authority in this instance referred instead to a *perceived* wisdom about moral matters that allowed for exceptional clarity.

The Stanford Encyclopedia of Philosophy[4] offers two definitions for morality, one descriptive (a particular code of conduct is adopted by a society or group) and another normative (emphasizing a universal or natural code understood innately by most humans). The "descriptive" version is obviously variable. Defined by social norms, religious precepts, or political edicts, it will mean different standards of behavior to different cultures. The second definition conforms more closely to what scholars and others generally refer to as ethics. Attempts to codify conduct in this manner include the

United Nations' Universal Declaration of Human Rights, created in 1948. As persuasive as this document is, we humans can still scarcely agree on what it means to treat each other with dignity, respect, and equal access to freedom and opportunity.

Even in our own country, we often become confused with definitions of morally acceptable behavior, which seems to mix ethics with more changeable political, religious, and social standards. We're unlikely to ever again find slavery permissible in the U.S., but we continue to argue about life and death; and these arguments inform our still-evolving laws concerning stem cell research, abortion, and euthanasia, as well as our considerations about homicide, the death penalty, and war.

Still, the optimistic among us believe, or at least hope, we're making progress. We may backslide, violate our own code of conduct, or on occasion rationalize our behavior in the name of expediency. We could point to the various Wall Street debacles as evidence that some of us may be blurring ethical distinctions and forgetting which lines should not be crossed. But we assume we know the lines are there.

Americans want to believe we're all about the greatest good. When well-intentioned people discuss America's moral authority, they're not thinking about something closed-minded and inflexible, but rather high-minded and noble. They're referring to the potential of our government and our leaders to use America's great power to achieve in a manner that is in line with our highest ideals. In the best of all possible worlds, we're employing the good kind of moral authority.

I'm skeptical about good moral authority. Making an ethically informed decision is a process to be emulated; however, it neither requires nor grants moral authority. Even a series of wise or well-considered decisions do not confer the sort of pure, "touched by an angel" variety of power implied by moral authority.

How is it we decide who has moral authority in America? How do we make that determination? Who are these reliable paragons of virtue on whom we can count to exercise this authority? How do we decide who has the moral muscle and who gets to flex it?

Steven Pinker, author and professor of psychology at Harvard University, noted, "Our heads can be turned by an aura of sanctity, distracting us from a more objective reckoning of the actions that make people suffer or flourish."[5]

To use his examples, we may believe Mother Teresa to be far more admirable than Bill Gates, even though it can be objectively argued that Gates' efforts to alleviate misery do far more actual good than did Mother Teresa's efforts at ministry. Not only that, Gates apparently offers aid without making moral judgments or imposing requirements relating to devotion. Yet many of us probably believe Mother Teresa had moral authority. We're struck by her aura of saintliness, her devotion, even her asceticism; we're inclined to believe those qualities made her a better model, even though there is evidence, as Pinker pointed out, that her well-financed missions featured far more emphasis on prayer than on advanced medical treatment.

We're susceptible to what I call moral charisma, which makes moral authority as much about the messenger as about the message – no surprise in our celebrity-conscious culture. We're as likely to be influenced by *how* someone says something or by *who* says it as we are by *what* that person is saying. This isn't a recent phenomenon; but the absence of more traditional institutional authorities in the age of mass communications gives more power to the clever and charismatic communicator, especially if he or she is espousing views we already hold.

That moral authority persists in a society as relaxed as ours probably seems a little odd; no one's the boss of us, after all. But moral authority's certainty has plenty of room to flourish in an atmosphere of intense divisiveness prevalent in contemporary American culture. We may occasionally elect a leader who believes in seeking out and listening to people who disagree with him, but that's not the way most of us operate. We tend less toward dialogue and more toward self-expression, and we seem more invested than ever in being *right*.

Having so many ways to bring our opinions into public discussion has been, on the whole, a terrific development. The Internet offers a window into the lives and thoughts of others; we can reach out in many directions to everyone from decision-makers to previously ignored or underserved audiences. We're exposed to different and unfiltered points of view. What better way to exchange ideas and perhaps even find consensus? Naturally, the Internet attracts its share of stuff that may be of value to no one (except family members) but we can always click away from the amateur art or the florid poetry. However, we're still faced with the challenge of knowing what information to trust. Even if we come to realize we're coming across an unsubstantiated statement or piece of gossip, it's already on view.

The Internet is a powerful tool for social networking. While this can create a strong sense of community, we can also become isolated from anything new or anyone who thinks differently. Spending time with people who think just like we do tends to exaggerate and harden our views.[6] Those views may become even more extreme because of "group think," and hanging around with (or reading or listening to) only those people with whom we are in agreement will prove that ours/theirs is the right viewpoint.

Knowing what is right is awfully subjective, particularly if we're basing it on something we know is true. Why? Because the brain plays tricks on us. According to Sam Wang, Princeton associate professor of molecular biology and neuroscience, and science writer and editor Sandra Aamodt,[7] our brains store information in the hippocampus but gradually transfer it to the cerebral cortex, separating it from its recollections about its origins. We won't remember how we learned what we learned, and we may not remember if we found out whether it was true or false. This means even if we learn something and we initially disbelieve it, our brains may forget we registered it as false. If we're not reassessing what we think we know, then we're going out in the world armed with as many misconceptions as proven knowledge.

My friends sometimes get caught up with emails containing warnings or predictions or fact sheets that turn out to be based on rumors or falsehoods. The website Snopes.com is dedicated to scoping out and debunking rumors that gain speed and stamina through multiple outlets. I don't know how they keep up, given how many of us are taken in by information that *feels* right, especially if it corresponds with something we already believe.

Not all ideas are equal – equally valid, equally worthy, equally verifiable. We ought to *know* that. It's just that sometimes we don't behave as if we do.

Lewis Black, a dazzling and dyspeptic comedian who has made a career out of raging, made this point brilliantly in the otherwise bland movie *Man of the Year*. Black played a comedy writer turned speechwriter for a talk-show host accidentally elected president (Robin Williams). His character spoke to the idea, so prevalent in the early twenty-first century's version of a debate or discussion, that any notion or thought is equivalent to any other by noting, "If everything is credible, then nothing seems credible."

He continued: "You know; TV puts everybody in those boxes, side by side. On one side, there's this certifiable lunatic who says the Holocaust never happened. And next to him is this noted, honored historian who knows all about the Holocaust. And now, there they sit, side by side; they look like equals! Everything they say seems to be credible. And so, as it goes on, nothing seems credible anymore! We just stopped listening!"[8]

Either that or we listen carelessly, not to mention selectively.

Giving everything equal time sounds as like a win-win situation. It's not. Some news shows present two unequally researched or reasoned points of view as equal. The viewer is left with the impression that an unreasonable argument is valid, or that someone whose viewpoint may have merit is foolish or confused. Furthermore, any presentation can be dressed up with "experts," flowcharts, and a great website. I wish we weren't ready to accept as true whatever seems attractive on the surface, whatever our friends like, whatever seems most dramatic, or whatever allows for an easy choice. Surely we're not that easily fooled, at least not if we're paying attention.

But we're not paying attention, not really. Our culture creates "junk thought."[9] Susan Jacoby, author of *The Age of American Unreason*, attacked our intellectual laziness, which she tied to our easy validation of ideas without merit. She pulled no punches in asserting that the United States is "now ill with a powerful mutant strain of intertwined ignorance, anti-rationalism, and anti-intellectualism."

This outbreak, she insisted: "...is inseparable from an unmindfulness that is, paradoxically, both aggressive and passive. [The] condition is aggressively promoted by everyone, from politicians to media executives, whose livelihood depends on a public that derives its opinions from sound bites and blogs and it is passively accepted by a public in thrall to the serpent promising effortless enjoyment from the fruit of the tree of infotainment."[10]

Alarms about anti-intellectualism aren't new and Jacoby's cautions seem to derive in part from a pronounced distaste for the way much of contemporary popular culture operates. Personally, I'm a big fan of pop culture (well most of it) and I'm not particularly worried about its corrupting influence as long as it knows its place and as long as we know it too. But pop culture does have a tendency to wander out of its lane. It's a little unnerving that world news seems to be covered by both CNN and *Entertainment Tonight* and that news anchors and entertainment hosts have begun to look and sound so much alike.

Nevertheless, the lines are blurred and there's probably no going back, which makes Jacoby's concerns relevant and our work that much harder. The election of President Obama, along with the enormous international and economic challenges that followed, seemed to inspire Americans to keep up with current events. But that may not hold. There's too much information coming at us too quickly. Who has the time to sort it out?

We often feel as if we're too overwhelmed and too tired to think. With ten- and twelve-hour days, long commutes, and family obligations, it may be easier to rely on others to point us in the right direction – too easy, actually. When I mentioned to a friend my concern that Americans display a depressing tendency to "follow the crowd," he replied, "Most people simply don't have the time to do the kind of nuanced thinking so many issues require."

Maybe we're so taken up by work, relationships, or keeping our heads above water that we *don't* have time to devote to issues outside our own daily lives. Maybe we're so anesthetized by all the equivalency that we accept by default whatever's most expedient. Or maybe we're so exhausted by what we're *supposed* to know that we can't be bothered.

More likely, we're unhappy with uncertainty. Uncertainty

leaves us feeling insecure. Polls taken by AP/Ipsos between 2003 and 2007 show a marked slide in the confidence of the American people, with a growing majority believing our nation was headed in the wrong direction.[11] While a poll less than six months after the 2008 presidential election showed a reversal of the downward trend in confidence[12] concerns about the economy, healthcare, and the possibility of war on multiple fronts may cut deeply into Americans' fabled optimism. Current events often leave us feeling helpless. We find ourselves glued to cable news, talk radio, or the Internet, trolling for solutions, seeking reassurance and comfort.

Comfort is available, in the form of charismatic spiritualists who are convinced they have answers to life's toughest questions. They may be self-styled spiritual leaders or modern-day advisers, but they're superior marketers. They never insist they have moral authority, only that they have access to proven methods by which we can individually or collectively come to understand that the best, or the most fulfilling, way we can live our lives will come from living as they suggest we do.

Neale Donald Walsch is described as a faith-based New Age spiritualist. Walsch enjoys an international following and is the best-selling author of several books. He preaches an inner-directed faith that allows for a personal way of communicating with God. He appears to simply offer suggestions as to how we can access our inner spirituality.

Walsch is not claiming moral authority. In keeping with other New Agers, he delivers a benign message, suggesting on his website: "Feeling is the language of the soul. Hidden in your deepest feelings is your highest truth. The trick is in getting to those feelings. I will show you how."[13]

It's a pleasant-enough concept on the surface, although a bit lacking in substance for my taste. Without a doubt, I prefer his approach to the hatemongers who preach exclusion and tout the likelihood that nonbelievers are going to hell. New Age spiritualism and self-help movements have always been more flexible and inclusive. Feelings *are* important, and emotions, rational or not, are a fact of most people's lives. But there's a subtext throughout Walsch's writing that makes me uncomfortable: thinking is something that gets in the way. Using the brain is toxic.

Walsch is selling certainty to uncertain consumers. Do this, feel that, listen to me, ignore the rest, trust me, you don't need anything else; there, you're all set. He succeeds not by force, but by marketing. Naturally, we aren't required to believe he has the only answers, or that his version of faith is the one we must embrace. So what is the harm of a Walsch or, for that matter, anyone peddling their version of certitude? We don't have to listen or follow their leads or acquiesce to their dictates. His brand of authority is moral, true, but it's also benign, unthreatening. Walsh undoubtedly feels he is on a mission to help people. He's also out to promote his books and lectures, and make money. It's a free country; why should we care?

We should care because what Walsch represents is a kind of moral authority packaged as the simple solution. Whether someone is peddling a better way to reach God or an unassailable justification for starting or ending a war, implicit in the message is the idea that the messenger (someone of good character or noble intentions) has already thought the issue through, saving us the trouble. He's certain; we're certain. Moral certitude is appealing, whether it's muscular or gently soothing, because it reflects confidence and strength of conviction. Confidence is good; I'd prefer that neither my doctor nor my president be wracked by self-doubt. But there's reasonably certain and there's the unflinching certainty of moral authority.

Why can't someone possess both moral authority and still feel doubt? This assumes moral authority is the appropriate term to describe someone with a set of admirable virtues, someone who might be open-minded or uncertain as well as, say, wise, compassionate, empathetic, or honest. But what makes them an authority? What lends their point of view credence?

The notion that moral authority is good and will be used for good in the hands of the right individual remains a powerful one in our cultural life. We bestow moral authority provisionally and remove it suddenly when we discover we've mistakenly chosen the wrong recipient; yet we're ready at the drop of a hat to hand it over to anyone – victim, hero, reformed sinner, or would-be saint – who can state with conviction, "It is so because I say so."

Chapter Two

THE NOBILITY OF SUFFERING

"Undergoing suffering isn't a virtue at all, and it's
unlikely to create any."

Susan Neiman—*Moral Clarity: A Guide for Grownup Idealists*

The stories of the September 11, 2001, attacks dominated the news
for months on end: tales about the heroism of the passengers,
the bravery of the first responders, and the courage of the survivors.
The event itself inspired a huge display of public sympathy and grief
here and around the world, magnified further by ubiquitous coverage
that highlighted the attacks, the devastation that followed, the shock
on the faces of ordinary citizens, residents, world leaders, and news
commentators alike. Everyone seemed to want or need to be part
of the wave of emotion that followed the attacks, which initially
manifested as a benevolent kind of red, white, and blue solidarity.
To counteract the disturbing sight of people dancing in the streets
of certain Muslim-majority countries, we had the Paris daily paper
Le Monde declare in a headline, "Nous Sommes Tous Americans."
(We Are All Americans.)[1] Meanwhile, U.S. citizens, many of whom
had previously viewed the Big Apple as foreign territory, suddenly
decided *they* were all New Yorkers, an identity people in and around

the city viewed with surprise but also with profound gratitude.

The media spun out various storylines: human interest, foreign policy, local heroism, or international response. The victims were remembered as "regular" men and women but also as martyrs or heroes in news accounts and on websites and makeshift memorials. At some point, the relatives took the place of the victims. These parents, children, widowers and widows, brothers, sisters and extended families of the dead numbered in the thousands and most were within reach of voracious local and national news outlets.

Others had suffered: the survivors, the Lower Manhattan residents forced out of their homes, coworkers and friends of the dead, and even those for whom the thought of an attack on American soil was simply too overwhelming to process. Rescue workers on cleanup at Ground Zero were exposed to toxic fumes while working twelve-hour days; charity agencies were swamped with requests and, within six months, thousands of military troops as well as inexperienced National Guardsmen were mobilized and sent abroad. Nevertheless, the families of the victims, those whose loved ones were killed in an unexpected terrorist attack upon the United States, remained, as a group, especially significant in the eyes of the public.

The closer to 9/11 one was, either by geography or personal loss, the more special one seemed to become. Various psychologists came up with a visual picture of "circles of affectedness." At the epicenter were victims' relatives. They were the custodians of their loved ones' memories; but they were something more: the proxy representatives of all those victims, regular Americans who went to work that morning unaware they would be brutally forced into a piece of American history.

Those further removed from the effects of the tragedy were somehow drawn to the inner circle of survivors in an effort, I suppose, to understand or somehow *know* the experience of being in the center of the circle. It was difficult to grasp how intensely interested so many were in the 9/11 families after the attack, harder still to see how desperately some people needed or wanted to get to know us. By and large, we were shown nothing but compassion. But some of our encounters were odd and occasionally off-putting.

Some people seemed to want attention by proxy; others felt free to confide in us. We received more than our share of calls, letters, and emails with advice, stories, problems, or conspiracy theories to pass along. I'm not certain why distant acquaintances or perfect strangers, for that matter, would believe it appropriate to burden a fragile group of people. Maybe they thought they were commiserating. I suspect they felt as if we who had suffered so much were in a position to more clearly understand their particular suffering.

We were continually asked to describe how we felt. I was never certain what that meant: how it felt to lose someone in a terrorist attack, how it felt to be alive but fearful and vulnerable, or how it felt to be part of a public mourning process while trying to grieve privately. We were able, some of us, to articulate how we were processing the relentless imagery of planes flying into the towers, people jumping, and towers collapsing again and again, along with pictures of the hole in the Pentagon wall or the crash site at Shanksville, but we could scarcely explain what it was like to know so much and understand so little. How could we really know *what* we felt?

It's probably human nature to try and make sense of what doesn't make sense; possibly people thought accessing our emotions would help them sort through their own. Those who sometimes forcibly inserted themselves into our lives may have imagined a kinship with the survivors or needed to feel as if they were connected more closely to the event itself. Maybe they thought that by knowing someone who was there or had lost a loved one, they could share more intimately in the communal aspects of mourning. Maybe they wanted to feel more a part of history. Perhaps they sensed that their primary question, "How could this have happened?" could be answered by those of us most directly affected. Yet it often felt as though people were rubbernecking at the scene of a horrible accident.

The media sought out and found 9/11 family members willing to talk about other issues: the success or failure of the charity outreach, the local and national government response, or the Victims Compensation Fund. What did we want to see happen at Ground Zero? And how did we think the rebuilding efforts should or could impact any memorializing at the site? What about the formation of a 9/11 Commission to investigate the events leading up to the attacks? What about its recommendations? Our responses were duly noted and often published, which was, to say the least, a strange and oddly heady experience.

All the attention was a diversion from the crushing sense of loss. I volunteered to become an advocate and moved back and forth between various communities and constituencies as need, experience, and my own energy level permitted. I knew these opportunities came from my "status" as a 9/11 widow. Invitations to join committees and boards, or attend meetings, sessions, interviews, and press conferences were based on my relationship to a victim, along with an assumption that I might be able to synthesize a 9/11 family member point of view. I quickly came to see there wasn't any such thing.

Being the object of so much attention was both healing and distressing for the 9/11 families. The significance attached to being a victims' relative at times overwhelmed me. I remember meeting a woman whose husband died a few months before mine. "I can't fathom what you're going through," she confessed. "It's not just the loss of your husband; it's the entire context."

Ah yes, the context: not just a widow but a 9/11 widow. Not

just a loss but a loss compounded by scale, by the fact that it was an attack on the nation and we were headline news for months. Then there was the anthrax scare in my community that had us wearing gloves to pick up the mail, or the color-coded terror alerts in New York and Washington that had us reconsidering subways and trains. The entire sequence of events required us to call upon hidden reserves of strength and survivor skills we might not have realized we had. I continue to be in awe of the suddenly single mothers who protected and sheltered their children as best as possible from the most serious effects of so much nonstop scariness.

Truthfully, we shared much in common with other victims of tragedy. Those victims or survivors mostly rise to the occasion, especially when supported by a sympathetic public. The experience changes us and sometimes (though not always) we're made better or stronger. Some have argued that tragedy builds character; I don't know whether I believe that or not. But I don't feel tragedy automatically confers moral advantage, and it certainly doesn't confer expertise. Yet somehow we – the press, the public, the family members themselves – colluded in the idea that something about our experience had rendered us exceptional.

The deference paid by the officials, politicians, and members of the press to our thoughts, opinions, and recommendations sometimes felt as if it bordered on reverence. As I heard references to the moral authority of the 9/11 families, I began to wonder whether it even mattered if our suggestions or objections were logical or illogical, informed or uninformed. Even the most outrageous demands were considered. In such an environment, how could we not feel as if our opinions were somehow deserving of special consideration because they came from us and we had, after all, gone through so much?

In an op-ed piece I wrote for *Newsweek* [2] about the reverence shown to us, I was steered away from using the term "moral authority" by my editor. Instead I gently suggested that the 9/11 families' grief didn't make us experts, an argument so obvious it bordered on ludicrous. Of course we weren't experts. We had insights, we had opinions, and we had an interest in helping and in making things better. But as the topics on which we were asked to consult grew to incorporate site programming, neighborhood redevelopment, national security, the reorganization of the intelligence agencies, or the Bush Administration foreign policy decisions, I felt as if efforts to include a 9/11 family voice (particularly when we were all starting to realize there wasn't a single voice that represented the thousands of relatives) was becoming far-fetched.

I wasn't implying that family members were uninformed or unable to make assessments, draw conclusions, or express opinions – far from it. We were widely divergent in terms of experience, education, background, and temperament. Some relatives were clearly more learned when it came to certain issues than others. All of us, however, had the option of becoming involved to whatever extent we wished.

Furthermore, the activities of the 9/11 activists have had lasting and, for the most part, valuable impact. The creation of the Commission and the 9/11 day of service, the efforts to develop treatment programs for traumatized children or reach out to other victims worldwide, the support for widows and school children in Afghanistan or soldiers in Iraq all represent a generous donation of time, money, and spirit by 9/11 families seeking to make the lives of others easier. Furthermore, the wisdom among trauma specialists is that activism is often an ideal choice for those who've gone through an ordeal: a way to heal by helping others.

But no, our grief didn't make us experts. Nor did our experience confer upon us some sort of moral wisdom that obligated decision-makers to heed us or gave us special insight into what was moral.

If the branding of the 9/11 families as morally special created a personal dilemma for me, watching a tiny group of relatives attempt to turn it into a form of identity politics was nearly insupportable. A few vocal family members began to behave as if this very public tragedy and their very public losses entitled their views to consideration ahead of all others. They marched into meetings with a sense that they were *right*. Being a public figure, which carries with it the opportunity to influence, requires a kind of calculation and is best served with at least the appearance of humility. But grief doesn't allow for calculation or nuance. It's not something most angry, injured people are likely to successfully pull off.

The more publicized activities of the 9/11 family members began to generate an ugly backlash that played out across the Internet, on talk radio, and even on the op-ed page of *The Wall Street Journal*.[3] Several media outlets appeared giddy over exploiting the public's compassion fatigue by portraying relatives as spoiled and ungrateful, a broad-brush approach that played especially well outside of Boston, New York, and Washington. New stories began to pile up about foolish and embarrassing escapades attributed to some family members who had benefited from charitable efforts. The spending (and dating) habits of a handful of women who'd been married to firefighters killed on 9/11 made better copy than the quietly heroic and ongoing efforts of two Boston widows to raise money for war widows in Afghanistan.

The nastiness was disturbing but not surprising. We Americans aren't kind to our victims/heroes over time, especially when they seem too attracted to the limelight, even one we so willingly provided for them in the first place. I suspect we come to resent what we see as their sanctimony, notwithstanding we were the ones to confuse their grief with some sort of righteousness born of grief – which is what happened to Cindy Sheehan.

In the summer of 2005, Sheehan, the mother of a soldier slain in Iraq, camped outside President Bush's summer compound in Crawford, Texas, to protest the war. She became the center of a debate fueled by a widely quoted phrase from a Maureen Dowd column in the *New York Times:* "...the moral authority of mothers whose sons were killed in Iraq is absolute."[4] Actually, Dowd, in her article, seemed to be making the point that if the Bush Administration was going to use moral authority as the justification for waging a war in Iraq, then surely the relatives of those who sacrificed their lives in that war should be seen as possessing the same authority. A valid argument, but it only reinforced my point that moral authority is not and can't be some impartial, ideal representation of what is right.

Dowd's subtle approach was lost on the cable commentators who discussed and dissected the validity of Sheehan's protest. They noted how dramatic her protest appeared, which seemed to be the point; she wanted to attract attention in order to make her views known. But the talking heads were intent on deciding whether Sheehan's moral authority permitted her to speak out publicly against the war in which her son died. One analyst wondered whether Sheehan's status as mother of a soldier killed in Iraq made her "untouchable."[5] That seemed unlikely, given the number of commentators on radio, TV, and the Internet who expressed no compunction about trashing Ms. Sheehan, using words like "manipulative" or even "treasonous."

The author and journalist Christopher Hitchens, writing for *Slate* magazine,[6] questioned whether the mere fact of grieving gave Cindy Sheehan or anyone else any kind of authority. Hitchens had been an avid supporter of the Iraq incursion and his questions carried with them the suggestion that criticism of the war by this mother was ill informed. While I didn't agree with that point, he did raise an interesting question: Who decided that grief conferred moral authority and what was that moral authority supposed to mean relative to Sheehan's anti-war protest? Was it supposed to make her stance more meaningful or relevant or true?

Back and forth went the discussion on the blogosphere. Some sided with Hitchens, suggesting moral authority would also have to be considered the province of parents of soldiers killed in Iraq who nevertheless *supported* the war effort (the original view expressed by Dowd). Others argued the *special circumstances* of Sheehan's grief – her belief, that she lost her son to an immoral cause – lent moral status to her protest.

I hated this particular discussion because I felt it took away from very real arguments to be made against the decision to engage in an offensive war in Iraq. Presenting the war as morally just put up barriers against the kind of intense scrutiny such a decision warranted. Packaging the invasion as compelled by moral duty and tying it – falsely – to 9/11 and my husband's death was offensive. I could sympathize completely with Cindy Sheehan's rage.

Does a grief-stricken mother have a right to rail against the loss of her son to a war she feels is wrong? Yes, she does. Most of us will agree that the feelings of those most affected by political decisions must be acknowledged. If the government or any other entity is tearing down our houses, running a highway through our communities, displacing our workers, or sending our children to war, we deserve to be heard. Decision-makers need to understand on some visceral level what their policies do to human beings and they need to be reminded there are real consequences to the decisions they make. Victim testimony is the basis for many wrongful death suits and violent crime court cases. To consider suffering is to humanize the law and allow justice to be compassionate.

However, we can sympathize, agree, or even disagree with someone's point of view without assuming his or her grief lends moral strength to that view. In fact, we must make that distinction, because the moral authority of the bereaved can be turned to very different purposes. How would the presumed moral authority of mothers of fallen soldiers who supported the invasion make their views more or less valid?

To take an example with which I am more familiar: one woman, the sister of a 9/11 victim, has been for a number of years an outspoken supporter of both the war in Iraq and the Bush Administration's overall handling of the "war on terror." She organized protests against proposed institutions at Ground Zero and wrote op-ed pieces criticizing plans to close Guantanamo Bay. I don't share her sentiments, but if we are to give a green light to moral authority, she is as eligible as is Cindy Sheehan. Actually, she's been far more effective in shielding herself from criticism even as she has been far more apparent about her agenda.

This much should be obvious when considering the presumed moral authority of sufferers: Grief isn't particularly ennobling. It doesn't automatically confer dignity or produce heroes, although individuals may act heroically in the midst of suffering. Grief is messy. Forget those pictures of the bravely suffering widow or the stoic parents. Grieving people are deeply wounded. They're incensed, impatient, and often impolite. If they were insufferable before whatever happened to cause their grief, they aren't likely to become less insufferable in the throes of their mourning process. I once heard from a sleep-deprived aid worker in tears because she'd been screamed at by a 9/11 family member who thought she wasn't trying hard enough to help. I told her to remember that if someone was an idiot (I used a much stronger word) before 9/11, then he was still an idiot after the fact.

Sometimes grief brings out the best in us, but it's just as likely to bring out the worst. Some of the finest people I've ever met are

9/11 family members; so are some of the biggest jerks. Certain people tested by grief and loss go on to do great things and they can be rightly recognized as inspiring people. But I'll warrant it wasn't their grief that made them special in the first place.

Nor does grief imbue them – or anyone touched by tragedy – with the divinity of suffering. I'm sure most of us would insist that seeing the victim as divine is not our intention. And yet, such a reaction may be ingrained in the American psyche. According to a Christian website I researched, suffering is a path to salvation, one that reminds us of our human frailty, causes us to turn to God, allows us to understand sin, helps us prioritize, grooms the soul for eternity, and engenders nobility.[7] Few of us, Christian or otherwise, willingly choose to suffer (although we will all eventually suffer the loss of a loved one) but when the suffering of others is judged by us to be particularly acute, many Americans seem to regard the sufferer as enduring something that makes him a better, more noble, and even more pure human being.

I suspect coming face to face with the idea that we're turning sufferers into saints would not make us particularly comfortable; perhaps that's why we're so quick to counter with the nastiness that has become endemic to our civic and public lives. We may live in mean-spirited times, but I do wonder if that's in part the result of our constant disappointment. In looking for someone or something to emulate, we too quickly set our sights on the exalted sufferers, only to be let down by the discovery that they can be as petty, angry, unforgiving, and inflexible as the rest of us. The public's mood shifts, patience wears thin, and icons learn that the high ground is treacherous.

Cindy Sheehan felt the love and then she felt the backlash. Much of this had to do with how particular opinion leaders, editorial page writers, bloggers, and others felt about the war. But an awful lot had to do with whether she was viewed as a righteous and noble mother or a treasonous manipulator. I saw her as a furiously grief-stricken parent, one who found her voice and used it. Her right to protest didn't need to be justified by anything except her anger and her citizenship in a country that allows for peaceful protest.

As I noted earlier, people assume a connection with the victims and survivors of a tragedy. When the tragedy is of a public nature, people may see the pageantry (for lack of a better word) associated with the occasion as a way of safely expressing emotions and participating in an event, as happened following the premature death of Princess Diana, or the shootings at Columbine or Virginia Tech. The intimacy created by the media narratives about those whose death is public may explain the intensity of our experience of those deaths. At the same time, we may venerate the survivors and want to get close to them to further understand their experiences. In the process of getting to know them, we're likely to support the efforts of various news outlets to turn them into temporary celebrities.

Turn on any morning "news" show and you'll probably come across someone talking about overcoming adversity. The stories are meant to be inspirational, and sometimes they are. Often, however, the victims, near-victims, and survivors have little or nothing to say, which makes it even more painful to watch them struggle with their conflicting emotions in full view of the audience. Their conflict comes from the awe, excitement, and appreciation they feel at experiencing the wave of attention "fifteen minutes" of fame brings. At the same time, they may be still dealing with the effects of shock or grief.

The survivors of large-scale events or dangerous incidents who suddenly find themselves in the limelight may very well know or figure out pretty quickly how to handle their public roles. They may be compelling storytellers and can even turn into extraordinary advocates. Others aren't and don't. Producers know all of this; they know soliciting sufferers, survivors, and victims might be manipulative or unwise in certain circumstances; it might even result in embarrassing or boring television. But that hasn't stopped them, as far as I can see, from trolling for stories of pathos as well as redemption, featuring victims or survivors, especially small children. Perhaps the victims and would-be celebrities know it, too, which is why a family impacted by tragedy is likely to show up at the television studio with publicists or advisors in tow.

A real celebrity has been defined as someone "who, by the very process of *living,* provide[s] entertainment"[8] and that's not what the victims/survivors are all about. Their unfortunate narratives are temporarily compelling enough to attract our sympathy or at least our interest. The media plays a role in presenting them and their stories as larger than life; we go along with it and often, so do the victims. To be the recipient of so much attention may be disorienting and confusing while coping with the consequences of a terrible occurrence, but it's also peculiarly empowering.

Still, fame is fickle, even for the mother of a soldier killed in Iraq or the daughter of a trader killed in 9/11. Those people who have experienced their own version of hell are apart from the rest of us; we sympathize but we also see them as special. We want them not to disappoint us. When they do, by being angry, defiant, self-involved, or maybe just boring, we lose interest. Disenchanted, we withdraw our attention from them, and allow them to fall back to earth.

Chapter Three

A Higher Authority

"The faith that stands on authority is not faith."

Ralph Waldo Emerson—essayist (1803-82)

The World Trade Center site was considered sacred ground by a number of 9/11 family members, particularly, I noticed, the relatives of the firefighters. I found it interesting and a little perplexing, insofar as the bodies of most of the rescue workers who perished at the site were recovered and buried elsewhere. Why was their place of death a sacred place? Would the same hold true of a hospital room, a highway, or a vast ocean? Nevertheless, the issue was a very sensitive one for those who felt the sixteen-acre area that defined the original World Trade Center footprint must remain empty. I didn't see things that way; Ground Zero was a killing ground, not sacred ground. One firefighter explained to me during a contentious meeting with planning officials that I couldn't understand because I wasn't Catholic.

True, I wasn't Catholic and I wasn't sure what Catholicism had to say about treating such a place where so many had died and so few (at that point) had been recovered. Since real estate considerations determined the site wouldn't remain empty, the philosophy behind the discussion seemed almost moot (although given the massive problems with rebuilding, one might imagine a cosmic payback is taking place). Still, the experience left me wondering about faith and certainty: surely it must be possible to support the idea of a cosmic presence without imagining there are answers to every question and a clear way of proceeding in every circumstance. Truthfully, I have no idea what God might have wanted for Ground Zero and that has nothing to do with my belief in some sort of higher power and everything to do with my doubt that I have a direct line into whatever that higher power is thinking.

Most Americans believe firmly in God, in whom they invest varying degrees of authority, a condition relatively unchanged throughout the course of U.S. history. According to the Pew Forum on Religion and Public Life,[1] which conducted a three-part survey in 2008, we are most assuredly a nation of believers, primarily Christian believers (seventy-nine percent), although there are more denominations and sects within that group than ever before. A clear majority of those responding to the survey said religion was a part of their daily lives. Notwithstanding the significant diversity of faiths and the fluidity of commitment to a particular practice (people seem to be moving around amongst various practices, trying to find just the right fit), Americans take their religious and/or spiritual selves very seriously. Among the sixteen percent who described themselves as unaffiliated, the majority believes in the presence of something greater. More fascinating still is that twenty-one percent of those who identified themselves as atheists also claimed they believed in God. This suggests that either there are powerful cultural incentives to feel a part of something larger or that these independent-minded souls have decided to redefine atheism and upend our ideas about belief.

How Americans think about their God was also the subject of a 2006 study by Baylor University's Institute for Studies of Religion.[2]

Instead of noting the denominations with which the respondents identified, the survey asked the participants how they viewed God and developed composite pictures of faith. This novel approach yielded some surprising results. More than half the respondents envisioned a very active God, directly involved not only with world affairs but also with everyday life. The interaction was seen as either benevolent or authoritarian, but it existed. The much smaller group that saw the supreme being as more distant was divided between those who saw God as less involved but still strict, and those whose God was less personal and more of a cosmic force than a constant and active presence.

Differing views about how active or how strict one's God is will likely result in differing attitudes about what constitutes moral authority, or who is assumed to have it. Since so many people rely on religion in order to come to an understanding about God's intentions, it may be worth remembering who usually has the responsibility of explaining or interpreting divine intention: fallible humans.

I'm reminded of a *New Yorker* cartoon in which a saint-like figure – with a halo – is fretting over a scroll he's writing. His companion appears to dismiss his concerns, saying: "Quit worrying about corroborating your sources – it's not as if anyone's going to take all this literally."[3] I sometimes wonder what divine being might have ever imagined that entire careers would be constructed around positioning oneself as the ultimate interpreter.

Fortunately, Americans are becoming more tolerant and less likely to take the word of their particular sacred text as gospel, so to speak.[4] In fact, the majority believes there are many paths to salvation; even those without religion or with shaky faith in God might find their way to Heaven. This benevolent point of view stands in stark contrast to the fundamentalist and fundamentally exclusionary interpretations of faith gaining strength in other parts of the world.

The more relaxed view of religion in America suggests that while Americans might believe in an involved God, they might also believe that humans are fully equipped to understand instinctively what God wants or expects from them. This in turn suggests the possibility that those that do subscribe to the notion of an activist God might also concede that those who don't – those with altogether different views of the universe – might still understand what it means to be moral without an authority to tell them.

In other words, regardless of how any of us come to know right from wrong, we are capable of being moral people and accountable for our actions.

Excellent, I say, because that opens up the tent to include all sorts of people with varying degrees of certainty about what lies above – or beyond. Whether we believe God to be ever-present, a distant cosmic force, or even a debatable construct, we can come together to create, adapt, and agree on a shared moral code that will guide us through our daily lives. Ethics and morality don't eliminate the possibility of faith; they simply don't require it. It's hard to imagine being more tolerant than that.

If only it were that simple!

The view that a man or woman with unconventional religious beliefs (or no religious beliefs at all) can be a moral person is still hard for many to grasp. In fact, tying morality to faith or lack thereof is still a favored pastime of the more conservatively religious. Such people seem to believe religion is under assault, which only strengthens their conviction that the moral fiber of our society is also under assault. It's hard to tell whether the authors, commentators, bloggers, and talk-show hosts sounding panic-stricken about the atheists or God-rejecters within our midst are sincerely afraid about a decline in values they insist is tied to a godless culture, or whether they are being deliberately provocative in order to gain fame, attention, and/or market share.

One of those provocateurs is Ben Stein, economist, commentator, star of several television ads, and briefly, host of a game show called *Ben Stein's Money*.

Stein's 2005 holiday riff on celebrity and God[5] continues to make the email rounds. The sincerely devout and the doubting faithful who keep it circulating contend there are some valid points buried within his lengthy commentary – and there are. He has an entertaining style, if one likes low-key and laconic, but something about this particular riff didn't sit well with me. I picked up a whiff of barely suppressed intolerance masquerading as concern for the good old days.

Some background is in order. At the time of this particular rumination, the marital woes of singers Nick Lachey and Jessica Simpson dominated the celebrity landscape, providing him with his point of departure: "A few confessions from my beating heart. I have no freaking clue who Nick and Jessica are. I see them on the cover of *People* and *US* constantly when I'm buying my dog biscuits. I often ask the checkers at the grocery stores who they are. They don't know who Nick and Jessica are, either. Who are they? Will it change my life if I know who they are and why they've broken up? Are they so darned important?"

Stein has a point about our addiction to the trials and tribulations of our celebrities. These people and the emotional train wrecks they occasionally generate seem to provide entertainment value outside whatever their talents are supposed to be. Truly our enthrallment with the details of their lives, especially when they're in a downward spiral, suggests we are prone to a spiteful streak of voyeurism. Then again, we also tend to slow down to look at traffic accidents.

Stein might have stopped there; instead, he continues: "Next confession: I am a Jew…I do not like getting pushed around for being a Jew and I don't think Christians like getting pushed around for being Christians. I think people who believe in God are sick and tired of being pushed around, period. I have no idea where the concept came from that America is an explicitly atheist country. I can't find it in the Constitution and I don't like it being shoved down my throat. Or maybe I can put it another way. Where did the idea come from that we should worship Nick (Lachey) and Jessica (Simpson) and aren't allowed to worship God as we understand (Him). I guess that's a sign that I'm getting old, too. But there are a lot of us who are wondering where Nick and Jessica came from and where the America we used to know went to."

His specific gripe in the above commentary was that some communities might ban Christmas trees in the public parks or schools if they thought it made others uncomfortable. I will allow that banning a decorated tree might strike some as over the top but I don't think it signals a distressing turn away from his kind of America, one in which we relied on God to define our values for us, instead of celebrities like Nick or Jessica or Britney or Lindsay. Rather, it's an effort to strike a balance between what we in America define as tradition and what the new version of our increasingly multicultural country might look like.

I'm uncomfortable with Stein's emphasis on returning to the good old days. The America we used to know was probably the one I grew up in, in which we all sang or were expected to sing Christmas carols in school, and social clubs were still segregated by religion as much as by race. I don't miss that America, to be honest, and I'm not convinced it's essential in order to protect us against atheism or whatever it is Mr. Stein fears. The Constitution takes the approach that the minority, not the majority view needs to be safeguarded. We may sometimes become overly invested in our efforts be culturally correct; in any event, people of faith are not the minority in this country.

Obviously Stein knows America is literally the farthest thing in the Western world from an atheist country, explicit or otherwise. When he bemoans the fact that he's not "allowed to worship God," he seems to be complaining about an America whose ship is morally adrift. His is not a new argument but it remains a sensitive one: lack of God in public life equals lack of faith, equals social breakdown, equals a society reduced to one in which mindless worship of celebrities (or other forms of moral depravity) are the order of the day. But it remains a potent one.

Of course Stein is exaggerating to make a point, but since I've received his Christmas tale almost every year since 2005 from various acquaintances, I suspect he's also struck a chord. There remains an ongoing debate about the place of religion in our public life. It comes up when we worry about placing a menorah next to the manger scene at the town hall, when we're considering a candidate's fitness to serve, or when we wonder how greedy executives became separated from a moral system that values integrity. Given the predilections of a majority of Americans, is it even possible to completely separate religion from the public sphere? On the other hand, aren't religious beliefs supposed to be private?

No they aren't, as anyone running for public office learns. During the 2008 presidential primaries, candidates were tripping over one other in their efforts to make a case for their devotion. Article VI of our Constitution says: "No religious test shall ever be required as a qualification to any office or public trust under the United States." But religion played such a significant role in the 2008 presidential contest, I had to go back and check to make sure I'd read the passage correctly. If we're not ready to elect a non-Christian president (and I don't think we are), we can be certain we're very far away from electing or even nominating anyone whose religion is less than completely familiar – and therefore completely unthreatening.

Much time and effort and news reporting were taken up with discussions about who had faith, and what kind of faith, during the presidential primaries. First, there was the matter of candidate Mitt Romney's religion (he's a Mormon). In a speech designed to assuage voters' concerns[6], he proclaimed his beliefs in common with other Christian sects and declared the country to be a Christian one while suggesting public life really couldn't be conducted without acknowledging the presence and influence of religion.

The candidates' faiths continued to be an issue even after the preacher who would be president, Mike Huckabee, dropped out of the race. Then Internet gossip insisted that Barack Obama was a Muslim, owing primarily to his exotic name and unconventional background. The rumor persisted (and persists) because we live in a time when Muslims are suspected of links to terrorism; no amount of appeals to logic (not that logical thinking is at work in this instance) will change certain mindsets for some time to come. It's weirdly ironic that this bit of false information was for a time overtaken by outrage over inflammatory remarks about race and America by Obama's Christian pastor, Jeremy Wright. The net result was that a candidate who was attempting to avoid ethnic or religious divisiveness was nearly swamped by it.

The 2008 primaries demonstrated that the candidates' faith and how they choose to express that faith continue to be significant factors in how Americans judge candidates for public office. That may be why Rick Warren, author of *The Purpose Driven Life* and the high-profile pastor of a mega-evangelical Saddleback Church, was able to persuade presidential candidates Barack Obama and John McCain to appear at Warren's church in August of 2008 and discuss how their (Christian) faith might influence their choices in governing.

We're told that knowing and understanding the faith of a man or woman running for office will give us insights into how he or she might make judgments. But what to make of a question asked by Warren of both candidates: "Does evil exist?" That question doesn't invite nuance; in fact, someone who has no trouble answering "yes" is likely to conduct foreign policy based on a very particular mindset.

If we're going to insist on questioning candidates' beliefs because we think those beliefs will inform their policy decisions, why not question everyone's beliefs? Austin Dacey, author of *The Secular Conscience*, argues that belief belongs in public life where it can "be held to the same standards as any other [claim of conscience]: honesty, rationality, consistency, evidence, feasibility, legality, morality, and revisability."[7] That would mean that a candidate like Huckabee or the eventual Republican vice-presidential nominee Sarah Palin would have needed to vigorously debate and defend his/her support of creationism as a plausible alternative to evolution, because such views could influence decisions about what is taught in public schools. The same would then hold true when we were considering candidates to become Supreme Court justices; to ask about their beliefs is not to be anti-religion but to try and understand how (do we even ask "if" anymore?) those beliefs might influence their interpretations of the law. An interesting proposition, but not one we seem ready to embrace just yet.

Religion was an issue when John F. Kennedy ran for president. At that time, the American public wasn't ready to trust anyone with the highest office in the land who didn't worship in one way and one way only. There was widespread concern that Kennedy might take his orders from Rome; some voters expressed fear that his allegiance to the Pope would supersede his allegiance to the American people.

Kennedy directly confronted the issue of how his faith might impact his leadership as president when he spoke in front of the Greater Houston Ministerial Administration in 1960: "Because I am a Catholic and no Catholic has ever been elected president, the real issues in this campaign have been obscured – perhaps deliberately, in some quarters less responsible than this. So it is apparently necessary for me to state once again – not what kind of church I believe in, for that should be important only to me – but what kind of America I believe in...an America where the separation of church and state is absolute... an America that is officially neither Catholic, Protestant, nor Jewish...For contrary to common newspaper usage, I am not the Catholic candidate for president. I am the Democratic Party's candidate for president who happens also to be a Catholic."[8]

How succinctly he seemed to put to rest any concerns about separating faith from politics and reminding voters that any elected official must do the same. One might have thought that after such a declaration we'd have accepted the idea that drawing a line between religious beliefs and civic responsibilities would be considered a good idea. Yet, nearly fifty years later, we're not there, which is to say: we're still here.

When Nicholas Kristof wrote a piece advocating an embrace of evangelicals during the 2008 campaigns,[9] the eminent storyteller and activist Theodore Bikel responded in a letter: "The issue is not the faith of a candidate for high office. The issue is that faith itself should be an issue at all...Largely because of the pressure exerted by evangelicals, every single candidate for higher office has been obliged to issue declarations of personal faith...Not that there's anything wrong with leaders who find the underpinnings of their moral and social conscience in their religious conviction. But to expect, let alone demand that people in high office govern as Christians (or Muslims or Jews – fill in the blank) is perilous..."[10]

Lewis Black also has a question about faith-testing our political leaders: "Since I don't have that much faith I don't really care if my leaders have much either but they constantly seem to want to show me just how religious they are and I don't care! I don't know when it got important for them to... discuss their relationship with God with me because I don't care! ...It hasn't got a thing to do with what makes a good president. My president can worship Ronald McDonald for all I care. I just want my president to have a moral center. That's what matters, doesn't it?"[11]

Does it? Well, yes, but apparently it's not all that matters. As Bikel and Black both recognize, Americans, despite having vastly different ideas about what it means to be religious, are afraid of people who aren't. How can such a person be said to have a moral center? Anyone who doesn't make a visible show of invoking God's name and following an identifiable religion (currently, Christianity or a benign form of Judaism) is suspect. We don't seem to trust anyone who isn't very publicly looking upward for support.

The anti-theism crowd also has its voices; writers like Richard Dawkins, Sam Harris, and Christopher Hitchens, who are far from subtle in expressing their distaste for God-centered belief systems. In their writings, they figuratively take a sledgehammer to various aspects of faith, religion, and God. Hitchens, in his best-selling book, *God is Not Great: How Religion Poisons Everything,* alternated between indignation and glee as he skewered several major belief systems in a sharply-worded style that left no doubt as to what he rejects and why he rejects it.

Hitchens' thesis that religion is the source of much of the world's sorrow is well-documented and his wit is on full display. At times, his acerbic approach can be off-putting.

Still, Hitchens makes what I consider to be a critical point when he declares at the beginning of his book that those who are not motivated by faith are nonetheless perfectly capable of being both ethical and moral: "Here is the point about myself and my co-thinkers: Our belief is not a belief. Our principals are not a faith... We do not rely solely upon science and reason...but we distrust anything that contradicts science and outrages reason...We are not immune to the lure of wonder and mystery and awe...We are reconciled to living only once, except through our children, for whom we are perfectly happy to notice that we must make way, and room. We speculate that it is at least possible that once people accepted the fact of their short and struggling lives, they might behave better towards each other and not worse. We believe with certainty that an ethical life can be lived without religion."[12]

I don't agree that we are required to accept our lives as short and struggling in order to behave better towards one another. But I applaud the way Hitchens endeavors to uncouple ethics and religion. Leading an ethical life doesn't require one to subscribe to any particular religion. Moreover, leading a religiously observant life doesn't guarantee by any means one is living an ethical one.

If the majority of Americans want to elect or appoint officials for whom religion or faith is central, then those Americans need to do more than accept that an affiliation with a familiar religion somehow guarantees good character or good leadership. We have to be willing and able to ask questions about how a particular set of beliefs might work with and for the public good. As for those leaders already serving, their version of God may be distant or active or nonexistent, as long as they don't assume their beliefs exempt them from being questioned when it comes to how they go about making decisions or judgments that affect the people they represent.

Throughout history, there have been men (and occasionally women) who have claimed to be acting on instructions from a supreme being. Because we're so reluctant to question beliefs, we seem to feel we aren't in a position to argue with someone who claims to know God's intent. Why not? When President George W. Bush and President Ahmadinejad of Iran both insisted they were getting their marching orders from a supreme being, we had to assume they were hearing two different sets of instructions and conclude that perhaps they were both listening imperfectly.

There are many versions of the higher authority and many ways in which Americans try to determine what those versions mean to them. No matter what our beliefs, however, our skepticism ought to extend to anyone who claims to act on a higher authority's behalf. Regardless of our devotion, we must be willing to question those who feels justified in interpreting God's private communications as giving them the moral authority to make momentous public policy decisions. As Madeline Albright remarked, "History would be far different if we did not tend to hear God most clearly when we think He is telling us exactly what it is we want to hear."[13]

Chapter Four

RIGHT MAKES MIGHT

"America can lead again, but we must restore our
moral authority."

Senator Christopher Dodd (D-CT), 2007

The attacks of September 11, 2001, were so devastating, so personal, and so unexpectedly shocking that they seemed to negate
any kind of nuanced response. We Americans believed the attacks
represented an assault on our way of life, on our freedom, and our
values. Sometimes it seemed as if we viewed ourselves as having been
exclusively injured, as if the awfulness of terrorism had not already
penetrated many corners of the globe. No matter; a great wrong had
been committed and action was needed to make it right. What that
action was occasioned some disagreement, but not much. Most people
couldn't have agreed more with our president when he said, "You're
either with us or against us." The situation was that clear.

Not to me. I saw the attacks as representing humanity at its
worst. Targeting civilians for death or commandeering them as part
of a suicide mission directed at others was wrong in every sense of
the word. I believed my husband had been murdered by terrorists,
not freedom fighters. But those terrorists were also dead. People were

clearly itching for the government to do something; but what? Go after the mastermind, Osama Bin Laden? Fine, do that. And then? Because as angry and shocked and devastated as we all were, I felt strongly that a measured response was the only response that made sense.

Some of my colleagues professed to be stunned by my hesitation to support an all-out war. One woman who had become completely unnerved at the thought of another attack got right up in my face not even a month after 9/11, screaming, "They killed your husband! You of all people should understand why we have to do whatever it takes to get these bastards." No point in asking which bastards she meant; she was ready to bomb the entire, unfamiliar, suddenly threatening Arab world.

She wasn't alone. While Americans seemed initially inclined to unite in the spirit of resilience, our political leaders were clamoring for retaliation. The focus was on the moral injustice of the attacks and the moral justifications for a "swift" response. The media were brought on board to deliver the message repeatedly and unequivocally. The emphasis on offensive action was in part a calculated bid to mobilize support at home for a series of foreign policy decisions while also sending a message abroad. But the approach also grew out of a black-and-white worldview promoted by those who envisioned the United States as having the moral authority to do whatever was necessary to eradicate evil.

William J. Bennett wrote a book in 2002 with a title supporting that worldview. In *Why We Fight: Moral Clarity and the War on Terrorism,* Bennett was incredulous that anyone could express any doubts whatsoever about our mission. He asked: "How was it that, in the wake of the bloodiest and most devastating attack on American citizens in our history, sensible and patriotic people could ask, 'Did we bring this on ourselves...' or 'If we go to war against them, does that make us as bad as they are?' ...that [those questions] could have been asked in all innocence... bespoke a deep ignorance about not only the rest of the world but more urgently and much more disturbingly about America. And it bespoke an even deeper want of clarity about the difference between good and evil..."[1]

The problem, in Bennett's view, wasn't the enemy, but weaknesses in America's moral understanding, which he tied in part to an education that fails to emphasize the superiority of American values in its attempts to support multiculturalism. Mostly, however, he deplored our lack of backbone. "Why were not more of us angry...?" he asked; "Why wasn't anger itself considered a moral response to unprovoked attack?"[2]

Bennett wrote approvingly of George W. Bush's revival of the language of good and evil. He lampooned the "sophisticates" who reacted with disbelief and horror at the president's attempt to "place our response on an unassailable moral footing."[3] In his view, hard-line anti-Americanism was indistinguishable from reasonable questioning. To make his point that American unity was countermanded with a homegrown anti-Americanism, Bennett used as examples provocative comments and writings from a left-wing coterie of academics, people he referred to as apologists for terrorism.[4]

It's true there were those who argued that the victims "brought the attacks on themselves." Colorado professor Ward Churchill caused an uproar with a widely circulated partial quote that described the World Trade Center workers as little Eichmanns.[5] Evangelist Jerry Falwell apparently blamed the attacks on a culture of permissiveness that included pagans, abortionists, feminists, gays, and lesbians.[6] Both the statements were outrageous, yet Bennett focused on Churchill's statement in order to launch an attack against "terrorist sympathizers." The group included those who were trying to understand the underlying ideology that motivates terrorism.

"The problem," in Bennett's opinion, "is not that Americans

are unpatriotic...The problem...is that those who are *un*patriotic are, culturally, the most influential among us."[7] I'm not sure what culture he's referring to; the vast reach and enormous influence of conservative talk show programs and hosts like Bill O'Reilly, Rush Limbaugh, and Sean Hannity were and continue to be a factor in American life. Those commentators had no problem after 9/11 labeling those who questioned the Bush Administration as unpatriotic, unappreciative, or even traitorous.

How could anyone believe that asking questions or demanding accountability of our government was unpatriotic and that those who did so didn't appreciate the great freedoms our country gives them? Didn't our Founding Fathers emphasize that the government was beholden to its citizens and the citizens were responsible for making certain the government was acting in their best interests? That sounds reasonable, but reason is often a casualty of fear, and fear was the order of the day: duct tape, gas masks, and gloves to pick up anthrax-tainted mail; confusing color-coded alerts that had us waiting for, if not expecting, an imminent attack.

We were at war against a shape-shifting target: one day a madman hiding in Afghanistan, then a rogue group crossing borders and operating independently of any nation-state, then suddenly a ruthless dictator in another Middle Eastern country without any clear ties to the 9/11 attacks. All of the targets were tied instead to our unending war on terrorism. To garner support, the Bush Administration cast the struggle in noble, heroic terms, which is how governments generally seem to mobilize public support. Selling a war can't be simply about politics, geographical advantage, or economics. The stakes have to be higher: freedom or justice or national defense. It helps if whatever entity is waging war can rely on a shared sense of identity that can be translated into solidarity for the mission.

America's citizens have in common that strong national identity, along with a tendency, "in times of crisis especially, [to] cast national challenges in religious terms."[8] Our battles become, in a sense, righteous struggles. It's easy to see how even an enlightened citizenry like ours might be made to believe doubt is unacceptable and certain acts are morally justified and thus beyond question. In this instance, moral authority resisted challenge and sanctioned the actions that led to the invasion of Iraq.

Madeline Albright's book, *The Mighty and the Almighty,* directly addressed the role of moral judgment in American foreign policy. While recognizing that questions of morality should and will enter into foreign policy judgments, she wrote, we still must determine what is moral and how much weight morality should carry, given other, more practical considerations.[9]

Albright had been accused of being ruthless during her service as secretary of state, a practitioner of pragmatic politics to the detriment of humanitarian impulses. She addressed the issue in later chapters, acknowledging the criticism that followed severe sanctions imposed on the Iraqi republic after the first Gulf War and expressing regret for the way she presented her decisions. But she is known to advocate a foreign policy approach that mixes realism and idealism. I was especially interested in her use of examples of what might seem to be good, moral decisions, such as support for refugees of ethnic cleansing, among whom were both victims and killers, to illustrate that "efforts to pursue an ethical course in foreign policy are frequently undermined by unintended consequences."

She continued: "To achieve moral results, a policymaker would have the conscience of a saint, the wisdom of a philosopher, and the prescience of a prophet. In reality, we stumble along as best we can despite shortcomings in all three qualities."[10]

Albright was forthright about the influences on and the limitations of trying to proceed on a purely moral basis when it comes to practicing foreign policy. A political moderate and a profoundly religious person, she made clear her belief that while church and state can and should be separated, religion is going to and should be a part of our public life. She warned, however, against casting any struggles as a contest between good and evil, especially since we could never say with certainty that anyone is completely good.[11]

Most Americans believe our country has been singled out for God's blessings, according to the results of a 2004 survey by the Pew Research Center's Global Attitudes Project.[12] That doesn't necessarily translate to belief in the moral authority of our country's leaders to conduct foreign policy but it's easy to see how some of those leaders might assume it as a given. Albright is less cavalier about such assumptions, noting wryly, "We have the right to ask – but never to insist or blithely assume – that God bless America."[13]

George W. Bush appeared to assume God was directing his decisions about the prosecution of the war. Whether he believed God gave him specific instructions or whether he was simply guided by God was a matter of some debate. Former Palestinian negotiator Nabil Shaath recalled that in a meeting in 2003, President Bush said to him: "I'm driven with a mission from God. God would tell me, 'George, go and fight those terrorists in Afghanistan.' And I did, and then God would tell me, 'George go and end the tyranny in Iraq,' and I did."[14] What is beyond question, however, is that the president of the United States was convinced he had been given the moral authority to make decisions about what actions to take to protect and defend our country. The moral nature of the authority granted, in his view by God, once again discouraged discussion or criticism.

It's entirely likely that all of our presidents believe in America's moral authority; the notion is ingrained into our political and cultural psyche. Our belief is not one shared by people living in other countries, however. The idea that America sees itself as special worries our friends and enemies around the world even as they note America's exceptionalism, its singular mix of history, government, and people. Exceptionalism has also come to have a more negative, post-Iraq connotation that equates it with an aggressive sort of American patriotism that exempts the United States from answering to international law.[15]

America *is* exceptional in that it is atypical. Think about it: so much space, so much freedom, so many diverse people bonded together by their belief in the ideals America represents, even if these ideals aren't always realized. To acknowledge that this country offers its citizens so much and has the potential to offer more, do more, and be more does not, we need to remember, mean that its leaders have the right or the obligation to claim moral authority. To want the best for American and world citizens, and to support their efforts to achieve a life free from terror, fear, or subjugation are worthy *moral* goals for our country. To assume our good fortune has rendered us morally superior and has given us permission to do what we wish is simply hubris.

We might imagine the view from abroad is – or at least was, before the election of Barack Obama – based on misunderstanding mixed with resentment and perhaps even a little envy. Europeans and others pointed out that while we Americans claimed to be willing to criticize our government's presence in Iraq, we nevertheless returned to power in 2004 the same administration we'd been criticizing. During a visit to an academic conference in Spain in 2005, my colleagues were all too quick to view the reelection of George W. Bush as proof that Americans, like their leaders, were primarily bent on some form of world domination.

We really aren't. Americans strongly support their country and what they fervently consider to be American values. But as the Pew researchers discovered, while Americans think those values might be good for other people, they aren't particularly interested in forcing the issue.[16] Aggressive democracy promotion is not something most Americans are interested in pursuing, preferring a more "take it or leave it" position.

The issue of whether America ought to assert its moral authority in global affairs remains a sensitive issue abroad. At the end of April 2008, the Royal Geographic Society of London hosted a debate on the motion: "America has lost its moral authority." As the *New York Sun* reporter Daniel Johnson observed, this might have been nothing more than an excuse to vent displeasure with America's diplomatic and military actions up to that point. Before the debate had begun, a majority of the audience had decided to vote for the motion. At the end of the debate, when the vote was taken, the motion failed, in part because of a vigorous defense that included a question posed by one American journalist: "America has ceded the high ground – to whom, exactly?"[17]

The debate hinged on whether any government, country, or entity other than the United States could claim moral authority. No one argued about whether moral authority was a legitimate aim for any government or whether such an authority might be required for a peaceful or just world. The point of the debate and of Johnson's article may have been to illustrate the depth of anger against the United States at the time but it also highlighted European ambivalence concerning the idea of moral authority. While European nationalism doesn't appear to have a religious component, I'd guess that many people in Europe wouldn't object to an America they could trust to help or protect them in times of trouble.

There was talk, following the election of Barack Obama, that we had entered a new political age, one focused on the renewal of public diplomacy and "soft power" (The term, coined in the early nineties by Harvard Kennedy School professor and former dean Joseph Nye and reintroduced in his 2004 book by that name, refers to using persuasion instead of force in conducting foreign affairs). The assumption has been that our political leaders won't attempt (at least in the near term) to formulate a foreign policy based on identifying and casting out evil; as Madeline Albright pointed out: it's a task that is "for mortals, an impossible job."[18] But I'm disconcerted to see that the term "moral authority" is still in play when it comes to discussions about America's role in the world. True, one would hope if America is going to set the bar in terms of global leadership, it had better be able to clear it and then some. But does exemplary leadership require moral authority? I think not.

Still, many political thinkers from the left, right, and center continue to see such an authority as a prerequisite for American engagement with the world. Some fear America's lost moral standing post 9/11 impacted humanitarian efforts to address regional famine or genocide, although those efforts have gone forward despite world opinion. Others are concerned America's battle against terrorism was compromised by apparent violations of international law. The implication – and sometimes it's far more than that – is that the restoration of America's real moral authority is tied to our renewed commitment to what used to be called truth, justice, and the American way. If we simply take that route, if we do what is good and right, we'll become once again the world's role model.

The central tenant of journalist Ron Suskind's book *The Way of the World* was a sort of "right makes right;" we win our way back to world leadership by regaining "the moral power that the world now desperately needs [America] to possess."[19]

Suskind's book was notable for its interviews with insiders who appeared to substantiate claims about the Bush Administration's efforts to suppress or ignore information in making its case for the Iraqi war. But Suskind's primary theme concerned moral authority, as he made clear during his appearance on *The Daily Show* with Jon Stewart: "The book is all about the fact that America's moral authority is bled away and [about] the need to restore it to fight the battles we need to fight – and the way you do it is with truth."[20]

Truth is a noble goal, one this nation fortunately gives us the freedom to pursue. But pursuing truth in order to restore moral authority presents a greater challenge. Will we really know when we've arrived at the truth – or The Truth? If we decide we're there, does that then give us moral license to do whatever we feel we need to do? Perhaps Suskind's "good" moral authority allows for doubt or debate, but my experience and observation suggest that people who believe themselves in possession of the truth tend to believe they're also in possession of the moral authority to act on it.

Critics who oppose the idea that American can claim – or reclaim – moral authority often insist that America has disqualified itself because of past misdeeds. That's the position represented by one side of the Royal Geographic Society debate and embraced by DC Rapier, a blogger who wrote after Suskind's *Daily Show* appearance: "...there is, regrettably, one 'Revelation' that Mr. Suskind has not experienced; that regarding the prevailing myth of American moral authority...The vain, prideful fantasy that America possesses intrinsic moral authority is both a ludicrous and harmful one. It has been used to whitewash the ruinous, foul effects of American foreign and domestic policy for centuries."[21]

The piece, posted on the progressive website OpEdNews.com, goes on to detail America's policy screw-ups, from "social injustice to the atrocities of war," before inserting this caveat: "Granted, the American people and American administrations have undertaken many noble, humanitarian projects. The premise being argued here is not that Americans are wholly without merit or virtue. The contention is that Americans, demonstratively, do not have the right to claim intrinsic moral authority."[22]

Although I dislike the idea of intrinsic American moral authority, it's not for the reasons DC Rapier presents. Our mistakes don't prevent us as a nation from behaving morally and being regarded as capable of moral actions. Ours is a country with a civic commitment to tolerance. The problem is that those who insist America isn't worthy of moral authority end up elevating the idea of moral authority itself. I'd flip that argument: The issue isn't whether America deserves or is worthy of moral authority, given its past history. Rather, the issue is whether moral authority is a worthy goal for America to pursue.

If we're hoping the world will look to America for moral leadership, we need to do what we do best: pursue truth, justice, and fairness to the best of our ability while remaining aware of our fallibility. We don't need – and the world will surely forgive us for not having – some sort of moral authority. What should matter instead is "…the attempt, messy and uncertain in its outcome…but handled according to established moral standards such as honesty and compassion."[23]

Chapter Five

CELEBRITY WORSHIP

"The cult of celebrity trivializes everything it touches."

Theodore Dalrymple—"Guided by the Stars"

While we've long debated the relative merits of religious or government-influenced moral authority, the contemporary version feeds off our belief in and addiction to the power of celebrity. I doubt most celebrities consciously see themselves as moral authorities. Practicing altruism, however publicly, isn't quite the same thing. But they're aware of their power and they have at their disposal high visibility, savvy marketing expertise, and charisma to spare.

Celebrities, according to cultural anthropologist Neil Gabler, are people whose lives have narratives we find interesting and entertaining.[1] Some of them are also smart, caring, and informed individuals. A few lucky ones possess such a potent combination of intelligence, compassion, charm, and star power that we see them as both reachable and yet apart – one of us who is not at all one of us. Celebrity informs so much of our culture that it's becoming almost impossible to separate it from other areas of endeavor such as scholarship, leadership, experience, knowledge, and sound judgment. Our culture has made the attainment of celebrity status the ultimate measure of success. One obvious reason is that celebrity translates into earning power. Whether someone is promoting her credentials as a medical expert or promoting his latest movie, the goal is to become a known quantity. Sometimes simply being famous is the goal; the hope of enrichment is deferred or even secondary to being thoroughly in the public eye. Having a video on *YouTube* seen by millions of viewers is the *ne plus ultra* even if we're also holding onto a day job at Old Navy.

A recent poll asked school-age children in Great Britain what they wanted to be when they grew up and about a third of them responded they wanted to be famous.[2] Maybe it's something that nine-year-olds say, but it was remarkable both for its lack of career specificity (remember when kids used to say, "I want to be a fireman"?) and for its clarity of purpose. It doesn't matter *how* one gets famous, as long as one gets there. The rest will presumably follow: attention, influence, money, and power. Given the myriad opportunities, fame as a career goal seems eminently attainable, if only for fifteen minutes, as Andy Warhol suggested. Education, experience, or talent don't seem nearly as important as timing, luck, determination, and a great marketing plan. It also helps to look good on camera.

If getting famous might seem within reach of millions, becoming a *bone fide* celebrity is out of reach for most of us. Still, the ranks have been swelling; once reserved for entertainers and sports figures, celebrity is also accessible to (and desired by) newscasters, politicians, writers, bloggers, and amateur videographers. The most bizarre aspect of fame is that it's sometimes granted to those who are known for...being known. How else to explain the early celebrity of a Paris Hilton? Even those who report about the famous can become celebrities. For sheer outrageousness (and occasionally witty zingers), witness the popularity of celebrity blogger and outsized personality Perez Hilton (no relation to Paris).

In such an environment, we're likely to admire the occasional celebrity who finds himself more amused than entranced by the strange overlap of fame into other areas. Television actor Dennis Haysbert, who has made a career out of portraying strong and reassuring authority figures, played the president of the United States on the enormously popular television show *24*. Haysbert finds that people continue to approach him on the street and urge him to run for office. "I don't know if it is a joke or that people just like to say those things," he observed in an interview.[3] Ironically, he believed his portrayal paved the way for the acceptance of Barack Obama as president.

Martin Sheen, another actor who convincingly played a wise president on *The West Wing* has been, throughout his life, an anti-war activist. He is thoroughly committed to his beliefs and apparently willing to inconvenience himself by occasionally getting arrested. Nevertheless, he doesn't fancy himself a potential legislator, let alone the leader of the free world. When asked to become a candidate for the U.S. House of Representatives from a district in Ohio, he turned down the offer. "I'm not a politician," he reminded his supplicants; "I just play one on TV."[4]

Can we tell the difference between an actor playing a character and the real thing? Maybe we can and we just don't want to; such is our desire to believe these characters will make better (and perhaps more moral) leaders than our real-life choices. *New York Times* columnist Frank Rich picked up on this sentiment in a clever op-ed piece in which he proposed we consider an adorable, kindhearted, and ultimately heroic trash compactor as excellent presidential material. "Wall-E for President"[5] may have been written to be tongue-in-cheek but it speaks to both our disappointment and our need for unadulterated larger-than-life figures, even cartoon ones.

Celebrities can be very effective spokespersons when it comes to causes. More and more stars seem to be interested in world affairs. Beyond the obvious publicity benefits of standing behind or in front of certain issues, some of these personalities sincerely want to make a difference. From Vietnam War protests to No Nukes and anti-apartheid concerts, from Band Aid and Farm Aid fundraisers to a focus on everything from global warming to genocide, childhood malnutrition, or the empowerment of poor women, celebrities have been unafraid to align themselves with activities directed at alleviating the world's problems. As anyone connected with philanthropic ventures will acknowledge, celebrity involvement is an enormous boon to fundraising efforts. Since the public is inclined to be on a first-name basis with our celebrities (hey, George; yo, Brad; Julia, over here!), we may feel as if we're friends with these stars. Friends can always ask friends for help.

That's not to say that celebrities don't have something to contribute; they most certainly do. Many times those attaching themselves to causes are likely to be educated, informed, or at least committed individuals with access to experts and the financial wherewithal to bone up on a particular subject. Organizations hoping to attract attention to a given issue could do worse than have Angelina Jolie appear at the World Economic Forum in Davos, Switzerland, conference or before a United Nations subcommittee on refugee status. It certainly focuses our awareness in a way that conventional leaders rarely do at such meetings.

A celebrity who is very focused on a particular issue can do the world a world of good. Actress Natalie Portman's micro-financing project, the Village Banking Campaign, seeks to launch 100,000 new community banks in the poorest parts of the poorest countries in the world so customers, primarily women responsible for supporting their families, might have access to capital necessary to launch businesses. Portman graduated from Harvard. She's no dummy, for heaven's sake. Acting is a fortuitous day job for her, one she no doubt enjoys, but one that also lets her concentrate on her high-minded and high-profile work on behalf of a neglected population. Why not?

The fact that we may now link celebrities with not just social awareness but also informed activism owes much to U2 lead singer Bono. Bono has moved from interested superstar to proselytizer for wiping out the debt of Africa's cash-starved countries. He's recognized for being well-versed and intensely pragmatic, approaching debt elimination as smart foreign policy. He's a dedicated advocate of the theory that freeing up cash flow that can be applied to immediate problems might well eliminate the resentment and unhappiness in the poorest countries that are often breeding grounds for terrorist groups.

The idea that a huge pop star would immerse himself to such an extent in the problems of Africa was once nearly impossible for government leaders and academicians to fathom. No more. Columnist Theodore Dalrymple noted in an op-ed piece about celebrity[6] that most young people know more about Africa because of Bono than because of anything they studied in school. One of Bono's partners, Bobby Shriver (a member of the next generation of the ultimate in glamorous celebrity/political families, the Kennedys), began GAP's Project Red, a successful marketing/fundraising effort that has further focused attention on Africa's problems and, hopefully, solutions. In a world of increasingly high profiles for activist/celebrities, Bono functions as a super-activist. Despite some setbacks that have kept the G-8 leaders at a recent economic summit from moving as quickly as he'd like (Bono apparently used some choice language to describe their sluggishness in making relief commitments), the singer's focused determination to draw attention to the plight of Africa's economic and healthcare systems has drawn widespread admiration.

In a laudatory article in *Time* magazine, Bono was applauded for the way in which he'd handled his profile, "…molding himself into a shrewd, dedicated political advocate, transforming himself into the most secular of saints, becoming a worldwide symbol of rock 'n' roll activism.[7]

Bono, the secular saint.

The somewhat more cynical Dalrymple pointed out, "[Bono's] authority arises from his celebrity, not from his knowledge."[8] That's not completely fair, since Bono spent years immersing himself in the issues and certainly developed more than a superficial grasp of the complexities involved. But even if his celebrity is the driving force behind the attention, is that necessarily a bad thing? Of course it isn't. Given the prevalence of stories about this celebrity's brush with rehab or that one's messy divorce, it's positively refreshing to have our attention diverted instead to the world's plights. And some of these people are making a difference. Bono has real clout and while he hasn't achieved everything he's wanted to, he's gotten world leaders to think about the global community and the responsibility of rich nations to help poorer ones. It's a win-win situation – as long as we understand we're watching a celebrity advancing a cause. The cause may stir within us feelings of moral outrage or a sense of moral urgency but hopefully not because Angelina, Brad, Natalie, or Bono say this is how we should feel. What they're doing, what they're supposed to be doing, is pointing out that we need to pay attention to the issue at hand, not to them.

Of course there's an element of self-promotion involved, even if it's because of the apparent need many celebrities have to be taken seriously, as well as their addiction to attention. Obviously they'd jump at the chance to weigh in on matters of consequence. Even those with the best of intentions can't deny the kick that comes with having their fans value them as intelligent people, not just talented or good-looking ones. Maybe it's asking too much of celebrities, who by definition have sizable egos, not to get too caught up in their own self-importance. But is it too much to ask that they be very mindful that we are also invested in *them*?

Time's profile of Bono seemed to imply that by supporting a morally worthwhile cause, Bono had come to be seen as having moral authority. I wonder. Certainly I wholeheartedly support social activism, and it's gratifying to see celebrities apply their considerable money, fame, charisma, and ego to causes larger than themselves. These people are without question to be admired. To be fair, there's no evidence Bono is positioning himself to be seen as a saint, secular or otherwise. If on occasion he gets demanding, impatient, or carried away with problem-solving or championing certain solutions, well, why not? He's used to having people pay attention to him.

Let's remember; celebrity activists are also celebrity actors, performers with all the requisite skills of persuasion, presentation, and public relations at their disposal. They're capable of manipulating us into excessive dedication if they choose, and if we are willing to be manipulated.

Those celebrities who draw attention to legitimate matters of moral urgency are to be commended. Our job is to make sure we distinguish between the celebrity and the celebrity's issue. The moral worthiness of the project should be separated from the moral worthiness of the supporter. That way, even if we suspect that our favorite famous person is something less than entirely selfless, we can still appreciate the value of the cause he or she supports.

There's no denying we're drawn to those we feel we can trust, albeit these may be people whose livelihood depends on their ability to be persuasive. This is true not only of attractive celebrities asking us to help them work for a better world, but also of those who offer us advice on how to live a better life. The most successful of these people are celebrities in their own right, not only because of what they're promoting, but also because they convey assurance, confidence and, yes, trustworthiness.

These advisers, therapists, columnists, and authors obviously have something to offer, something people deem valuable enough to pay for. Most of us pick and choose from among the products and services they promote. We'll swear by this book or that Internet site, this business model or that lifestyle, this method for timesaving or that method for staying fit. Usually, our perfect yoga instructor isn't our savvy financial advisor, and our wise financial advisor isn't our insightful relationship counselor. None of us assumes there is one person who is so in tune with, in possession of, and connected to absolutely everything we might need to know about how to live the best possible life that he or she can do almost anything and seemingly do no wrong...unless that person is Oprah.

Arguably one of the most well-known, most influential celebrities in America (if not on the planet), Oprah Winfrey is not just a person or a television personality, but a conglomerate or even, depending on your point of view, a way of life. The tagline for her website is "Oprah.com is your leading source for love, life..." The line trails off in the search engine, but I imagine it might read "... and anything else you can possibly imagine." Millions (and they are mostly women) agree, turning to the television show, the magazine, and the aforementioned website for tips, hints, advice, and wholesale philosophies that will make their lives more complete.

One of the most fascinating aspects of the Oprah phenomenon is that it combines some of the tenets of New Age spiritualism with an outward-looking humanistic approach. Get yourself together, Oprah preaches: fix your body, your mind, your finances, your surroundings, your relationships. In short, fix your life. Then get out there and help others. Pay it forward – not a bad message at all.

Oprah has sought to expand her sphere of influence in ways

that inspire both awe and not a little nervousness in some observers. She is credited, via her book club, with jump-starting or in some cases reviving the careers of writers, and in sparking a renewed interest in reading, at least reading those books she thinks we should read. She is the authors' champion, although she could conceivably become their worst nightmare. Such was the case for James Frey, whose memoir *A Million Little Pieces* she enthusiastically promoted until she discovered it contained some significant exaggerations and outright fictions. Her on-air excoriation of Frey, who came on the show to apologize, is a classic. It's also a sign of her immense influence within the publishing industry that a recognized author would submit himself to a tongue-lashing by a talk-show host. It should be noted she later apologized to Frey for her harsh dressing-down.

In January of 2007, Oprah began an online seminar with Eckhart Tolle, author of the best-selling New Age book, *A New Earth*. Later that year, she opened a retail store in Chicago (The Oprah Store) that sells a mix of inspirational and informational books, various themed items, and even slightly worn clothes from her closet. The proceeds of the store go to charity. In early 2008, she launched a reality show called *The Big Give*. The show, which billed itself as a training session in the art of philanthropy, sounded like a terrific idea at the time. It was lambasted by critics but still attracted enough viewers to warrant a second season.

Oprah has consistently ranked among the most admired women in the world.[9] That would seem to allow for an extraordinary amount of influence in matters of the heart, the mind, and the spirit, not to mention, the political. Some have argued it was her support for Barack Obama and her appearances in Iowa just before the caucuses that pulled women voters away from Hillary Clinton and propelled him to victory in that state. If true, Oprah demonstrated some serious clout. After all, Obama's win subsequently mushroomed into a series of primary victories and the Democratic nomination for president of the United States. By the way, chief among Oprah's reasons for supporting Obama was that she was taken with his apparent moral authority, according to a report on NPR.[10]

Actually, it's the question of *her* moral authority that seems to intrigue and worry observers. Some have suggested Winfrey's influence takes on quasi-religious overtones, as a 2006 article in *USA Today* pointed out.[11] The author quoted a professor at Reed University who wrote two papers on Winfrey. She likens Oprah to a "hip and materialistic Mother Teresa" and had written, "Oprah has emerged as a symbolic figurehead of spirituality." A 2004 survey about Oprah on Beliefnet.com that was also cited showed thirty-three percent of 6,600 respondents said Winfrey has had "a more profound impact" on their spiritual lives than their clergypersons. Those numbers suggest a certain degree of influence.

But is it moral authority? Or maybe the question is: does Oprah think it is? Do her fans?

The critics apparently do, and they seem very worried. She strikes fear into the hearts of the radical Christian evangelicals, who appear flabbergasted by the obvious popularity of her humanistic/spiritualistic approach. One Internet evangelist has called Oprah "the most dangerous woman in the world" and derided her as a "New Age witch."[12] Some have argued that by holding out the promise of spiritual fulfillment without the concepts of sin or salvation, she is leading Christians on the road to Hell; others have labeled her as anti-Christian because she suggests there are many paths to divine knowledge. That Oprah's open-ended views reflect the beliefs of a majority of the general population must drive some of her religious foes crazy.

Oprah-bashing is also popular with writers and bloggers. For example, her television show drew the ire of a *Hollywood Reporter* critic whose scathing review attracted as much or more attention than the show itself. He criticized *The Big Give* as Oprah's bid for sainthood, labeling it a "profoundly hyperkinetic and unwieldy adventure in Oprah-as-Messiah hype" and then added: "Shallow as a birdbath, the program would appear to exist less as a true philanthropic exercise than yet another self-aggrandizing vehicle in Oprah's divine quest to become synonymous with all that is virtuous, good on Earth. We might well refer to this as *Touched by a Talk Show Host*." [13]

Most of these critiques can be dismissed as the rants of paranoid religious extremists or evidence of the typically snarky reporting common to much of what is called entertainment news. But others have expressed concern about Oprah's influence when it comes to pitching particular products or ideas. One example that drew widespread attention and criticism centered on her enthusiastic embrace of the philosophy put forward in *The Secret*, a book that drew large numbers of fans and more than its share of detractors.

A hugely successful best-seller that enjoyed world-wide fame, *The Secret* is a self-help tome that suggests if we visualize good things, good things will come to us, not exactly a new idea but repackaged as "The Laws of Attraction." Simply put, we'll attract what we project. If we think of ourselves as wealthy, we'll be wealthy. If we picture ourselves as powerless, we will be. Oprah was obviously taken with the idea that whatever we put out in the universe, whether positive or negative, would come back to us. She gave the book an enthusiastic endorsement, devoting two shows and several magazine articles to its promotion.

The Secret, say the critics, makes misleading and sometimes false claims to back up its proposition and places heavy stress on material gain and financial success. More troubling, it takes its message of blame too far. While viewing oneself as a victim can be debilitating, no good purpose is served by insisting that those battling cancer, dealing with abject poverty, or facing institutionalized repression have brought their troubles on themselves.

Yet certain readers have insisted on taking the book's message, explicit to begin with, as the absolute truth. One of Oprah's viewers wrote in to say that after watching the shows and reading the book, she was going to stop her breast-cancer treatment and use only positive thoughts to help in her healing. Oprah, to her credit, addressed the woman directly on her next broadcast, pleading with her to resume treatment. She also used the occasion to "clarify her thoughts," suggesting to her viewers that the Laws of Attraction might not be the answer to everything.

We could be excused for rolling our eyes and shaking our heads and exclaiming, "Oh please! Does Oprah really have to explain that? How crazy can her critics get?" However, *Slate* magazine writer Peter Birkenhead argued: "If you reach more people than Bill O'Reilly, if you have better name recognition than Nelson Mandela, if the books you endorse sell more than Stephen King's, you should take some responsibility for your effect on the culture. [Otherwise] the most powerful woman in the world is taking advantage of people who are desperate for meaning, by passionately championing a product that mocks the very idea of a meaningful life."[14]

Clearly Oprah, whose goal is to reach out, support, lift up, and empower women, doesn't believe victims of rape or abuse or genocide or those afflicted with infirmities, painful conditions or fatal illnesses, are simply victims of their own negative energy. In fact, her influence is derived in part from her championing of women and children in hopes of connecting them to a better life, whether that means losing weight, buying the right pair of jeans, seeking support in raising an autistic child, or leaving an abusive spouse. Her perceived moral authority comes from her enormous appeal and apparent devotion to her message of individual empowerment.

That's the problem. Because her audience trusts her so completely, and because they trust her motives, they may take her suggestions to heart, good, bad, inaccurate, or misunderstood. If Oprah says it's good, it's good.

Oprah is undoubtedly aware of her enormous influence, but does she think of it as some version of moral authority? I've never met the woman but I imagine there are calculations that have gone into creating her public persona. She's incredibly charismatic and clearly a smart businesswoman; she's also a mega-celebrity. For all intents and purposes she appears to be emotionally invested in her message of fulfillment. While she doesn't demand we follow her, she is marketing as strongly as someone like Neal Walsch.

Furthermore, she can be fervent in her embrace of certain views, products, and ideas. Oprah is never more formidable than when she combines an apparently heartfelt conviction with the natural star power that is the hallmark of brand Oprah. Even her monthly magazine column "What I Know for Certain" becomes an anthem of sorts.

Assumptions concerning Oprah's moral authority seem to emanate not so much from her fans but from those who are disconcerted by her ability to tap into the *zeitgeist* and by her ubiquity. I'd guess most of those who are watching or listening to, or reading, or taking classes with, or giving money to, or accepting money from Oprah can separate the hype from the helpful. I can't guarantee that a handful of those who admire Oprah might not confuse her goodwill with some sort of exalted moral supremacy. But I'd also suggest that her critics have a troubling tendency to sound like moral authorities.

When all is said and done, we're not always going to be able to separate even the most thoughtful of celebrity do-gooders from their egos, their desire for attention, their devotion to their careers, and their attraction to the spotlight; these attributes factored into making them famous in the first place. That they are seeking to share some of their largesse is more than admirable, and I'm certain that some of them may have something besides their money and their personas to share with us. The involved celebrities may be exceptionally gifted, exceptionally clever, exceptionally dedicated, or all of those things. They aren't, however, exceptionally blessed with the authority that demands we regard their utterances with unquestioned reverence.

Chapter Six

The Doctor Is Out

"The authority of medicine is the authority of science,
not of morality."

John Lantos, MD—*Do We Still Need Doctors?*

My dad's doctors weren't national celebrities but they were
very well known locally. Over the years and especially after
the loss of my husband, his beloved son-in-law, Dad struggled with
a series of cascading medical events: liver problems, a thinning
intestinal lining that resulted in constant bleeding, a blood disorder
contracted in the hospital, and a devastating skin condition. Although
he was hospitalized nearly two dozen times over five years, he was
able to live and finally die at home.

As my father's condition worsened, I spent more time in
Florida with his various healthcare team members. Most of them
were wonderful, caring people, but Dad's primary care physician was
brusque to the point of obvious impatience. I knew managed care ate
into the time the doctors were able to spend with their patients, or
with family members. I knew we patients and family members could
become demanding. But I had also run into doctors who appeared to
resent questions but felt free to express opinions about their patients

and *their* choices. And when Dad's doctor once said to me, "You know, your dad brought this on himself with his lifestyle choice," I had to keep myself from reaching across the desk and smacking his arrogant face.

Not the best example of a mutually trusting relationship.

Yes, my dad had cirrhosis, among other ailments, and cirrhosis is most commonly associated with alcohol abuse, although there are other causes. Dad was never drunk or abusive or forgetful or even sick. He lived a "typical" 1950's and '60's lifestyle, which is to say martini lunches and Scotch before dinner. Maybe it caught up with him in old age. Maybe he'd always had a weak liver. I honestly don't know.

I couldn't help wondering why the doctor made the remark. What purpose did it serve? Was he trying to get me out of his office? Was he trying to tell me my dad didn't *deserve* sympathy ("he's made his bed; now he'll have to lie in it"?) Was the doctor making a moral judgment? And most disturbing of all, would his attitude affect my dad's care?

I wanted my father to switch doctors, but he wouldn't hear of it. He felt strongly that at such a critical and vulnerable junction in his life, change would be risky. That's not uncommon with elderly people. Dad didn't seem to care about patient empowerment or the details of his illness or treatment. His doctor, he told me, was a professional. Fine, but was it too much to expect less arrogance and more empathy?

Doctors tell us they're losing power; one of my doctors is chronically late and blames it on a too tight schedule and various other administrative demands. He might have a point. But what kind of power do they need to regain to practice effective medicine?

Once upon a time, we gave to the men and women we called healers any kind of authority they wanted – cultural, social, moral.

While the priest or holy man interpreted the mysteries of the universe, the shaman, the medicine man (or woman), or the country doctor explained and treated the mysteries of our bodies. Certainly their knowledge of the complexities of the human systems seemed divinely inspired. The one person in the village who was able to get rid of a toothache, or suck out the venom of a poisonous snake, or apply a poultice to ease a fever was naturally the one who was revered.

The moral authority of the doctor-healer was cemented tightly by the approval of the clergy in the nineteenth century.[1] The doctor was thought to be a highly moral man who chose a noble profession and tended to both the physical and spiritual needs of his patients. The image of the kindly, attentive doctor of impeccable character (and paternal inclinations) seems to have survived right up through *Marcus Welby, MD,* a popular TV show in the early sixties. Even the surgeons of the pioneering TV doctor shows were heroic, although Ben Casey's brusque manner may have inadvertently cleared the way for a later television doctor and anti-hero, Gregory House.

Given our continuing fear of and confusion about life and death, it would stand to reason the professionals who make or help us make such decisions would still be held in high esteem. But experts believe our perceptions have changed. Jonathon Imber, in his 2009 book *Trusting Doctors: The Decline of Moral Authority in American Medicine,* tied it to a number of factors: doctors' increased involvement in addressing chronic diseases, which are frustrating to treat; the rise of a more bureaucratic and impersonal healthcare delivery system; the advent of innovative technologies and medicines; and the growth of patient-acquired knowledge and autonomy.[2]

Both Imber and Dr. John Lantos, author of *Do We Still Need Doctors?* have explored the changing role of the doctor. At one time, the physician's power derived from interpreting and intervening, but Lantos wrote that "...doctors no longer learn or understand or explain the meaning of illness or suffering."[3]

I doubt current and future generations of information-savvy consumers will put up with rude or moralizing behavior from a doctor the way my dad did. I certainly wouldn't. Maybe we don't respect our doctors as we used to; we're apparently less inclined to trust them. According to a recent Johns Hopkins study in *Medicine*, one in four surveyed believe their doctors subject them to unnecessary risks.[4]

Besides mistrusting our doctors, we're angry with them. Tara Parker-Pope, who writes on wellness for the *New York Times*, invited reader comments on her blog with her blunt assessment that, "The once-revered doctor-patient relationship is on the rocks."[5] She referenced the many "what your doctor won't tell you" books currently available and the fury expressed by patients on the Internet, as exemplified by one *Times* reader who wrote on Pope's blog: "I, as patient, say [to the doctor], stop acting like you know everything. Admit it, and we patients may stop distrusting your quick off-the-line, glib diagnosis."[6]

His anger may be tied to fear. Many patients, particularly if they are sick or old or otherwise vulnerable, are psychologically as well as physically dependent on their doctors and on the doctor-patient relationship. We may logically know our fate rests as much in the hands of the latest technology or the newest pharmaceutical release as it does with the doctor who performs the operation or recommends the drug. But we still rely on our doctors for expert advice and for help in making the difficult decisions. Moreover, we often hope and even expect they can work miracles. Lives are at stake.

Do we expect a full-time physician and part-time miracle worker to be morally certain about her recommendations, or simply more intuitive about and responsive to our needs, regardless of how harried, unsure, overwhelmed, and frustrated with the system she might be? Is it true that, as Lantos noted, "We are just not sure anymore whether we want doctors to be all too human or imperfectly divine"?[7] Maybe we want, and we want the system to support, a doctor who will be as honest as possible without being indifferent or brutal, will share information, and will listen to us as we express our fears about our health and our lives – or the quality of those lives.

Almost every medical decision seems to involve quality of life, not just because we seek treatments for chronic conditions, but also because life can be prolonged with varying degrees of assistance. Sometimes the decisions we need to make about our acceptable quality of life are, if not simple, then at least possible for us to make. When my orthopedist asks me if I want to consider ankle surgery or if I think I can wait until ankle joint replacement becomes more common – say, ten years from now – he is asking me to weigh the discomfort of having a weakening and unpredictable ankle joint against the risks involved in surgery. Since I'm able to make this decision on my own, there's no moral judgment to make, only a practical one.

But moral judgments come into play when deciding about what constitutes an acceptable quality of life for someone else, especially when the alternative is death. End-of-life issues are often vague; many people are concerned that decisions might end up in the hands of hospital or insurance bureaucrats, or even the government. In 2009, opposition to a public healthcare option caused widespread panic by focusing, somewhat misleadingly, on the possibility of a government-run "death panel" that could decide whether an older person received life-saving treatment or not.[8]

Even if a patient is competent to make his or her own medical decisions, our fear that someone might be aided in dying "before his time" remains. Euthanasia remains illegal in the vast majority of states. One of the most notable proponents of assisted suicide is Dr. Jack Kevorkian. Kevorkian saw himself as being in service to patients who were clearly able to articulate their needs and desires. Until he was arrested and jailed, Doctor Death, as he was called, gained notoriety for defying both the law and the medical community in order to help people end their own lives. These patients had determined that their medical conditions made their lives unbearable. They, and Dr. Kevorkian himself, believed they were exercising the freedom to define an acceptable quality of life. Others argued Kevorkian was taking advantage of mortally ill or somehow diminished people in order to make a name for himself. Even if the patients are considered competent to make their own determinations about ending their lives, suicide is still seen as an affront to God's authority to bring life into the world and to call it back.

The level of anger directed against Kevorkian revealed much about our discomfort with medicine and how we think it should be used on our behalf. Yes, he had the annoying aspect of a crusader and was virtually a caricature of the know-it-all doctor. But what most upset his foes was his offer of help to patients seeking to alter the course of nature He was, in some people's eyes, playing God or at least thwarting God's will, never mind that it was a choice his patients made.

The ongoing debate about euthanasia represents a fascinating twist on the separate but parallel ideas of doctor and/or patient empowerment and about who has the right, moral or legal, to end a life. In August of 2009, for example, a fatally ill man living in Montana filed a claim against the state, arguing that laws preventing him from seeking doctor-assisted suicide violated his constitutional rights. The case pitted libertarians and liberals against some disability rights groups, Roman Catholics, and evangelicals.[9]

The idea of God's will undergoes some major moral twisting

in traumatic cases, especially when life can be extended, however artificially. Most of us don't want to see our loved ones die, especially in unexpected circumstances and especially when they're young. We'll hope and pray and, for a time, close our ears and our minds to medical evidence that indicate life has ceased. After all, unexpected reversals have been known to happen. But apparently, it's not just some amorphous miracle we're expecting. An eye-opening survey on end-of-life medical care reported on CNN revealed many people still believe that God's intervention can reverse an outcome deemed hopeless by the doctors.[10] Doctors are often asked to prolong a life by any means possible so divine intervention can take place or so that the miracle can occur. Not only don't we trust the doctors' determination as to when to cease and desist, we don't even trust ours.

The notions of patients' rights and medical integrity can come into conflict or even be subverted, as when patients' representatives (family or friends) choose to fight for life or ignore existing "do not resuscitate" orders put in place by the patients themselves. The conflict indicates a shift in decisions about who is most qualified to determine what is best for the ill or dying person. Fearful of lawsuits and divested of the absolute authority they once had, doctors and other medical professionals are caught in a quagmire that often pits their years of training to evaluate available medical evidence against the family's belief that a miracle may be at hand. That these two viewpoints are neither scientifically nor (if it comes to the patient's best interests) *morally* equivalent is increasingly lost.

One of the most compelling – and repelling – doctor characters on television is the irascible Dr. Gregory House, the protagonist of Fox TV's enormously popular medical drama. House, played by the talented Hugh Laurie, is supposed to be a brilliant diagnostician as well as an exceedingly flawed individual. A self-pitying bully addicted to Vicodin for an old injury, he's a kind of anti-doctor – technically and analytically superior but supremely clueless and deliberately mean-spirited when it comes to relating to the human condition. He lacks any trace of empathy or the kind of mentoring and nurturing skills one might want from a doctor working in a teaching hospital. He routinely flouts ethical and budgetary considerations as he runs through one test after another in his quest for the correct diagnosis. House never doubts that all the poking and prodding and prolonging of pain is in the best interest of his patients who serve as his lab rats. The show's dynamic comes from our discomfort with his unorthodox methods, his lack of empathy and his overall character, even as we are attracted to his borderline insanity and corrosive humor.

The fans seem to love House's willful disregard of authority. Probably most of us find the character's situation fascinating, if implausible. Although House is clearly in it to demonstrate his brilliance, we're meant to admire his adherence to his own moral code. He's responsible not to the petty dictates of the hospital administration or the emotional whims of dysfunctional family members but to *the truth*. Never mind that he's a misogynistic, pill-popping, alienated S.O.B. whose behavior periodically crosses various ethical lines. We have a soft spot for the alienated loners; besides, we know he's interested in saving lives at all costs – although, for the patient, the costs may not be worth it.

Dr. House doesn't exist in real life, nor could he in the context of the healthcare business. No hospital could afford to risk its reputation or its economic stability on the presumed brilliance of one diagnostician. If the legal advisors to the board of directors didn't get him bounced, he'd almost certainly be overruled on a regular basis by a team of staff bioethicists. His bedside manner isn't simply atrocious; it's nonexistent. On the other hand, he never quits and he never gives up and most patients' relatives can be assured that he won't let *his* patient die as long as he even suspects there's a possibility that patient can be saved. If Dr. House is thinking about quality of life, he doesn't mention it. If he's thinking about medical futility, we'd never know it.

In real life, doctors struggle with defining "medical futility," which involves not only medical and economic but also moral issues.[11] Do doctors have a right to decide whether a treatment is worth it or not? Do doctors have the moral obligation to offer futile treatments? On the other hand, do patients, or more to the point, their surrogates, have a right to squander needed resources and force a physician's complicity? In this age of patients' rights, the medical profession will often cede to the family, although this can present another dilemma for the doctors or the hospitals. When family members can't agree as to the best course of action, the decision about whether to prolong or end a life can fly out of the hands of the doctors and the families – and into the courts or even the legislature.

The case of Terri Schiavo may be our culture's most prominent examples of how complicated society's views are concerning what it means to be alive. Schiavo, a forty-one-year-old woman, had been in what doctors diagnosed as a persistent vegetative state for fifteen years. She was breathing on her own but was sustained by a feeding tube. When her husband Michael sought to have the tube removed, her parents objected, arguing that she was conscious, medical evidence to the contrary. They believed Terri could hear and see, that she retained awareness, and that she might return at some point to a fully awake state, either by medical or divine intervention. Absent a living will, the family members argued about whether Terri would have wanted to continue living in such a state.

As Schiavo's parents sought to keep her alive, the case attracted media attention and both sides initiated legal and emotional appeals to state and eventually, national legislators. To Michael Schiavo and his supporters, shutting off the feeding tube was about ending measures to artificially prolong a life of someone who was insentient – absolutely unaware of anything and anyone and unlikely ever to return to consciousness. To Schiavo's parents and their supporters, removing the feeding tube was nothing short of euthanasia. This wasn't something the doctors were going to be able to decide – and ultimately they didn't.

The case bounced back and forth between the courts and the legislature, ending up in Congress, where Senator Bill Frist of Tennessee, a non-practicing physician, famously inserted himself into the controversy by diagnosing Terri Schiavo as sentient without visiting her. At one point Terri's feeding tube was removed, then surgically reinstated, then removed after the Florida Supreme Court granted Michael Schiavo's petition.

What worried me was where Terri Schiavo's doctors were – or weren't – in all the arguments. They obviously weren't considered to have any moral authority with respect to this case; that struggle was waged between members of the family, the press, the legislature, and various interested groups. But even the doctors' *medical* authority was questioned and their diagnosis doubted. They seemed to be marginalized, which bothered me. If we're going to debate what it means to be alive (does it involve being aware or being able to swallow, being able to breathe or being able to think?) doctors might not have the last word. But they must have some say in decisions about their patients. Their expertise has to be viewed as valuable, as essential. Otherwise, I worry that they may invest less in the outcome.

In Florida, it seems doctors are now erring on the side of caution, at least to hear my good friend tell it. In the summer of 2008, his father-in-law suffered a massive heart attack while playing with his granddaughter. Efforts to revive him were heroic; a heartbeat was established only after four tries.

As his wife's family waited in agony, my friend wrote: "It's been two weeks, and things seem to only be getting worse, in that he's stuck in Terry Schiavo-land. Doctors all say it's extremely unlikely he'll ever wake up – he moves his head from side to side and opens and closes his mouth, but there's nothing behind those eyes – no recognition. *The family is united* [italics mine] in believing he wouldn't want to live this way, but the doctors say there's still some chance – extremely remote, infinitesimally small, but still "a chance" – that he could wake up in a week, a month, a year, or ten years. Most likely he would be extremely impaired – living out his days in a nursing home – but still, technically 'alive.' My wife and her family need closure, and our priority is making sure her mother is okay, but the state of Florida has laws that, among other things, pretty much ignore living wills. So here we are, stuck in limbo."

If doctors' recommendations aren't considered and if families who are united in trying to honor a dying patient's wishes can't prevail, then the Schiavo case has left us with a truly awful legacy.

Because of the complexities inherent in any medical decision wherein technology makes it *possible* to extend (or end) life, a new field has been developed to deal with an array of non-medical ramifications that might be associated with medical decisions. Called bioethics, the field has evolved as a multi-disciplinary endeavor that takes into account not only moral and ethical issues, but also the relationship between medical practice and theology, sociology, science, law, politics, and economics. Applying a cost/benefit ratio to a sick or dying patient may seem cold, but it's a fact of life and it has ethical underpinnings, namely, where can the available resources do the greatest good? It may seem odd that it takes a village of philosophers, economists, biologists, sociologists, administrators, theologians, and lawyers to deal with knotty questions of medicine and ethics. Then again, it takes the onus off the doctors to try to figure out what it is we expect them or will allow them to do. The painful paradox about medical advances is that our technological options give us not only the freedom but also the responsibility to make the right decision, especially when we are making it for others who can't. Sometimes we don't have time to consult with all the interested parties. Certainly battlefield doctors don't; neither do any physicians or nurses practicing under emergency conditions.

In 2006, Louisiana Attorney General Charles Foti brought manslaughter charges against Doctor Anna M. Pou and two other nurses who had been working at Memorial Medical Center when Hurricane Katrina hit New Orleans two years earlier. Dr. Pou and her skeletal staff had stayed on in the aftermath of the storm to care for patients at the hospital, which was without power for days before help arrived. The three were accused of administering a "lethal" morphine cocktail to critically ill patients. The doctor insisted she was trying to make the patients comfortable, but the attorney general's office suggested she had taken matters into her own hands. A grand jury decided not to indict, citing the horrific conditions as well as the staffers' limited choices.

Although medical professionals generally applauded the decision not to hand down an indictment (civil lawsuits by the families are still moving through the courts), questions remain. What is considered to be appropriate treatment during a major crisis? Since most of us who weren't there can't imagine the chaotic conditions under which the staff worked, the idea that Dr. Pou should have tried harder to evacuate the patients might seem to be patently absurd. What could anyone have done?

On the other hand, doctors know that morphine, especially in combination with other drugs, can cause death. According to a *New York Times* article published near the fourth anniversary of the event,[12] the investigations discovered a large number of patients had lethal doses of drugs in their system. Could they have been evacuated? Was any effort made? A doctor's first directive is to do no harm, but what does that mean under these circumstances? Were the exhausted medical staff – untrained in decision-making in battlefield conditions – doing what was best for their patients by not attempting to move them, by assuming they *might* die if they remained? Were they deliberately killed in order that they not suffer a slow and agonizing death? Who has the moral authority, if anyone, to make such a call?

It strikes me (and scares me) that we're in the middle of a "throw out the baby with the bathwater" moment in the medical profession that the experts haven't got their expert arms around. Doctors may have lost some autonomy and may be required to depend on others to sort through increasingly complex choices.

As Lantos reminds us: "Autonomous doctors create problems. They practice in idiosyncratic, uncontrollable, and often irrational ways. They don't follow rules. They don't regulate themselves well...They have a medieval-guild mentality."[13]

So there, House.

I do want my doctors to feel free to act if they need to, using whatever knowledge they've accumulated and whatever expertise they can bring to bear. I need them to be able to confidently render medical advice based on their experience and their studies. But I also want them to acknowledge on occasion that they might not have all the answers or that they might have made a mistake. Owning up to medical errors has been difficult for doctors; the rising number of malpractice claims has threatened their livelihoods. However, over the past decade or so, hospitals and healthcare conglomerates have begun to embrace the concept of voluntary transparency as a way of dealing with wronged patients. While the notion may seem calculated as a way of preventing lawsuits, indications are that being forthright goes a long way in reducing patient and family members' emotional distress.[14]

Signs point to a team approach in our medical future. In this model, most of the listening and some of the explaining to patients is done by physician assistants, nurse practitioners, counselors and/ or therapists (depending upon the specialty). Larger practices have been implementing this approach successfully for years, primarily in order to cut costs by sparing the time of the most expensive team member (the doctor). While I respect the talents of the various professionals who make up my team, I want to have an opportunity to communicate with the person who is making critical decisions about my care.

Our expectations of our doctors remain high; I wonder at times whether most of us really do understand they are not divine. The advances in science and technology have convinced us doctors not only know what to do in any given situation but always have the power to do it. It's unfair of us to expect that of our doctors, and it's dangerous for our doctors not to disabuse us from that belief. Doctors deserve our respect; but they don't require or benefit from our belief in their infallibility.

Lantos asked: do we still need doctors? Of course we do. Their training and experience allow them to assess, deliberate, explain, make difficult decisions, and perform intricate medical tasks. Theirs is an authority born of expertise. But it is not a moral authority; in the unlikely event they might know everything about medicine, our doctors will never know everything about the *moral* implications of a judgment. Our trust in our doctors – and we need and want to trust them – will come not from our belief in their near divinity but in our conviction they are listening to us, advocating for and partnering with us, and that they will apply their medical knowledge to helping us even when there are moral consequences.

Chapter Seven

IN NEWS WE TRUST

"I would not know how I am supposed to feel about
many stories if not for the fact that the TV news
personalities make sad faces for sad stories and happy
faces for happy stories."

Dave Barry—American writer and humorist

I've always admired reporters. At one point, I actually wanted to
be a reporter. They seemed to be men and women of integrity:
smart, resourceful, and independent. Think Pentagon Papers or Deep
Throat. I'm a baby boomer and my view of the fourth estate was
romanticized by the belief that reporters would keep us all honest
because, when it came to reporting, they were all about truth.

My post-9/11 experiences have changed my view somewhat. I
did meet some top-notch journalists who were both careful researchers and compassionate reporters. But they and their colleagues were
at the mercy of their editors or their producers, who were themselves
at the mercy of some fixed corporate idea about what version of the
9/11 experience would be marketed. I noted primarily two kinds of
stories: the "how do you feel" or "how are you doing" stories, which
gained traction especially on and around the anniversary of the at-

tacks; and the conflict stories, where the tension came from the 9/11 relative's anger with charities, government agencies, public officials, and even, on occasion, other family members.

In both approaches, I soon learned, the thrust of the story had already been established. This was particularly true of appearances on cable shows, but even the local newspaper reporters knew what they wanted out of us. One time I was interviewed for a story about how difficult things were presumed to be for 9/11 families. The reporter wanted pathos, but my ever-changing mood wouldn't cooperate that day. Because moderately upbeat wouldn't do, he repeatedly brought me back to the horror of that day until he had me in tears, at which point the photographer began snapping pictures of my distraught expression. Another time, I was scheduled to talk about how well 9/11 families were coping – not *how* we were coping but how *well*. In that instance, I wasn't feeling happy enough to address the topics of healing, new romance, or the elusive feeling of closure. The interview never ran.

The ultimate negative experience was my turn as a guest on *The O'Reilly Factor*, not because of any philosophical or political differences I might have had with the cable star, but because I was felt I was duped. The topic, the producer assured me, was charity outreach, and whether or not it was working. I felt there were some failures and also some successes; I wanted to address both. After talking by phone to the producer over the better part of a week, I truly believed I'd be able to talk about problems and solutions. I probably should have known better, but I wasn't thinking clearly.

When I sat down in the studio just before airtime, makeup primed and hair in place, I overheard O'Reilly discussing with the other young 9/11 guest how angry she must be at a particular charity that hadn't yet distributed funds. His ire was directed in particular at George Clooney's efforts to produce a fundraising concert for the charity. That was the focus of his program: to prove Clooney and company had disgracefully cheated needy 9/11 families. I knew next to nothing about the specifics of that concert, I admitted with a smile, but I was happy to talk about how we might improve the bureaucracy that made it so challenging for the families to get help. O'Reilly returned the smile and informed me that bureaucracies existed on 9/10 and would exist beyond the current problems; they just weren't something anyone could do anything about. He then began the show by introducing me as a hurt, confused, and angry widow cheated by the charity supported by Hollywood liberals. I'm certain I looked every bit as stunned as he meant me to look.

I became increasingly careful as time passed, interviewing less and less. Producers and editors were disappointed I wasn't coming across as angry or controversial or passionate. I was once dismissed as "too nuanced" by a producer planning a panel discussion about some 9/11-related issue; she wanted me to come down for or against, and I wanted to look for common ground. I was passionate about not bickering, about finding the balance between competing interests, and about coming up with solutions. I made every effort to lift my deliberations above the high tide of my own emotions. But that didn't seem to be what the media was after. What my brief turn in the spotlight revealed is that journalism was journalism was – and continues to be – more about point of view (POV) than ever.

When the TV commentator Tim Russert died in 2008, Kurt Andersen called it "the decline and fall of serious-minded, voice-of-God mass media."[1] Andersen, author and *New York Magazine* columnist, noted that Russert was seen as a link between the "objectivity" of the older network anchors and the POV favored by the newer commentators. That Russert, formerly a Democratic operative with no formal training or reporting experience before his stint on *Meet the Press,* came across as the soul of objectivity speaks to the changing nature of television journalism. While the supposed objectivity is what once gave those "voice of God" types their aura of authority, their ilk is vanishing from the airwaves. Highly opinionated semi, quasi, and pseudo-journalists now dominate television, fighting for attention with webzines and citizen bloggers. As Andersen points out, the old newscasters almost never delivered opinions and the new ones do so all the time.

Andersen complained that audiences didn't know the difference between reporters and commentators. Perhaps he's right and perhaps that's why he occasionally gets flack for being opinionated even though, as an op-ed columnist, that's what his job is all about. Then again, the media is on shaky ground when it comes to trust. Even the august *New York Times* found itself dealing with not one but two journalistic scandals post-9/11 contretemps: Judith Miller's articles about Saddam Hussein's alleged weapons of mass destruction and the plagiarism attributed to its one-time rising star, Jayson Blair.

According to a 2006 report by Pew Research's Project for Excellence in Journalism, "since the early eighties, Americans have come to view the news media as less professional, less accurate, less caring, and less moral."[2] The survey also found that "seventy-five percent of Americans believed that news organizations were more concerned with 'attracting the biggest audience,' while only nineteen percent thought they cared more about 'informing the public.'"[3]

While specific outlets do appear slanted (i.e., *Wall Street Journal* represents a conservative point of view, *Boston Herald* a liberal one), two University of Chicago economists writing on perception of media bias concluded that newspapers adjust their slant to maximize sales. The bias or slant we might assume is dictated by the editors is in reality based on the identified preferences of the readers and is thus driven by the consumers.[4]

"The nature of the [news] business is commercial,"[5] noted

former *Harper's Magazine* editor Lewis Lapham, who had nothing good to say about the media in his scathing book, *Gag Rule*. His fury was directed at what he perceived as the spineless reporting about Bush Administration activities after 9/11. He emphasized that expecting the truth from those who give us our news is foolish. After all, we're in an age where entire marketing campaigns are built around something called perception management, which is a fancy way of saying you present to the people something you want them to accept or believe, irrespective of whether or not it's true.

A number of respected newspapers and magazines *have* staked their reputations on in-depth research and thoughtful analysis; unfortunately, those are in danger of disappearing, at least in print form. Many of the larger daily papers have content on the Internet and many have begun to charge subscription rates equivalent to those collected for print versions. The *Times* has made itself available on its own electronic reader and on Amazon's Kindle. As these versions become easier and more convenient to read, the bigger outlets might be able to hold onto their audiences even while moving away from print versions entirely. That's assuming, however, that their audiences not only believe content from the *Times* or the *Wall Street Journal* or the *Washington Post* is superior to content from alternative sources, but also that they believe it's worth paying for, even if they have to read it online.

As more and more reporters are laid off – people with training and experience – some are asking if the quality of news reporting will suffer. I wonder if it will matter to most Americans. We're already inclined to get our information from headline feeds and story summaries. We can also go to online news sites, where original stories by a skeletal staff and dedicated volunteers are supplemented by op-ed pieces by guest columnists. News reporting, like so much else in our cultural lives, has become about satisfying niches. In the past, we've gravitated to the print sections that interest us; now we log on, skim the headlines, and follow the links to the specific stories that interest us, ignoring the rest.

Whatever ends up happening to the news we read, it's likely to remain more in-depth than the news we watch. The broadcast networks, also struggling against multi-faceted and ever-changing means of information delivery, have downsized their news divisions. The networks still offer versions of evening news but after nearly half-century, the format shows signs of wear and tear. Many people have probably caught the lead stories online, which means any reporting squeezed into the segment is perfunctory and not particularly revelatory. The half-hour is predictable: the anchor person behind the desk or occasionally at another location begins with the lead story, followed by a health story (unless the lead story *is* a health story), followed by some sort of profile, which is then followed by human-interest story. One can switch back and forth between channels and see virtually the same lineup. There have been attempts to update the format, as well as the sets and even the studios. But fewer viewers are tuning in.

Americans still watch television; some studies have indicated they're actually increasing their viewing time, although they may be simultaneously surfing the Internet.[6] Viewers might catch CNN at the gym, Fox at the auto repair shop, or MSNBC at the local bar, competing for their attention with ESPN, but they don't' seem as interested as they once were in the "voice of God" commentator. Nor, in the age of Internet headlines, do they seem at all interested in network morning news anymore, which may be why the *Today Show* has become more about cooking, shopping, and tips for organizing everything from finances to closets.

Cable news shows also compete for viewer attention, offering their audiences not so much more variety as more volatility. This the commentators provide with head-wagging, eye-rolling, voice-raising, and frequent displays of righteous indignation. Analysis, when it is offered, barely disguises a very pointed view, often with partisan overtones. Some of the controversy appears as scripted as a wrestling match, presumably in order to be more entertaining. Viewers may be weary of the histrionics, particularly when they involve vitriolic rivalries between commentators that seem completely divorced from straight reporting.

The Internet is more than ever our source for news, especially as it becomes easier to access the Web with nearly any device from nearly anywhere. We already have access to far more information than could ever be presented to us in a half-hour news show or a print paper. It may be beside the point to ask if getting our news this way represents an improvement, since there's probably no going back. In many ways, the news delivery system is better – potentially.

Al Gore, well-known champion of the Internet, finds it to be "a nearly ideal medium for individuals with common perspectives and concerns to find one another and form communities around their shared interests."[7] He's absolutely right; anyone can find like-minded individuals, from dog owners to bicycle enthusiasts to cancer survivors to the isolated elderly. As any Facebook aficionado knows, it's possible to reconnect with friends or acquaintances from ten, twenty, thirty or more years ago. But just as we decide which communities we want to join and which friends we want to make or find, we're the ones who will determine not only what news is important to us, but also if what we're seeing is accurate, thoughtful, balanced, or carefully researched. The Internet will sort information for us based on what it perceives our interests to be, but it won't decide on the quality of that information, at least not yet.

The Web provides an opportunity to dig deeply into the substance of a story. It may not substitute for on-the-spot reporting, but it allows us to hear from the people who live in the locales where an event may be taking place. They may not be professional reporters but they'll be able to provide context. These aren't people we used to be able to reach, especially if they lived in repressive societies; in fact some still risk retribution simply by logging on and posting. But they persist and their perspective is critical to understanding what's really going on in other parts of the world.

Sarah is one of several people in their twenties I interviewed in an effort to find out how the next generation is getting its news and how that might affect its decision-making processes. Do they trust the available news sources? Do they feel they are as informed as they can be? Do they care?

Twenty-seven-year-old Sarah is hardly a typical young adult; she's a post-doctoral candidate at Princeton who is more traveled, intelligent, curious, and deeply committed than most people I know. She is focused on world affairs. But like many people under forty, she gets all her news online – not from television (she doesn't own one) and not from newspapers, which she views with a skepticism not uncommon among her peers. In that respect, she's representative of her generation, at least based on informal conversations I had with others in her age range about how they stay informed – or as informed as they feel like staying.

Sarah's particular beef with mainstream media is that the interesting global stories aren't covered, or they aren't covered in depth. She uses the Internet like a detective, tracking down original sources behind the stories she's most interested in. She'll often begin with a news aggregate like *Google News*, which she favors because it shows *how* stories are being covered. To delve more thoroughly into an international story, she looks for blogs that connect her to other blogs written by what she calls "firsthand narrators" in a given part of the world. Sarah acknowledges that while there is a great deal of information online, her contemporaries tend to read stories that reinforce their political perspectives or deal with topics of interest to them. Still she finds the Internet to be a vastly superior way to acquire information.

Rita is one of the busiest young women I know. A twenty-nine-year-old entrepreneur with her own physical therapy practice, she works ten- to twelve-hour days and at least one day a weekend. In addition, this married Indian-American woman is part of a tight-knit social group whose activities keep her occupied every available hour not taken up by work. Rita finds newspapers and their online counterparts to be frustrating. She feels the stories assume knowledge she might not have, that there's simply not enough time or space given to context, and that there's no follow-through. She suspects editorializing is substituting for objective reporting. Given her time constraints, Rita doesn't spend much time on the Internet, either.

That's not to say she isn't interested in what's going on around her, just that she has to find creative ways to keep informed. She tries to read magazine articles when she commutes into the city once a week to teach. She generally gets her news in sound bites from her husband, her patients, and her friends, who also send her links to web-based stories they think might interest her. This group also supplies Rita with their analysis of the news, which she seems to trust as much, if not more, than what she might get from mainstream media. Are her friends (including me) more qualified (or less qualified) to sort through and choose her news for her than the journalists hired by the editor reporting to the publisher answering to the media conglomerate owned by the even larger corporate entity? Hard to say, although we might certainly be under less pressure to censure or edit our thoughts.

Aaron is a twenty-five-year-old landscape architect and new-lywed living in suburban Maryland. He reads the *Washington Post* because, he admits, it conforms to his viewpoint, i.e., slightly left of center. He finds broadcast correspondents to be frustrating. He gets the bulk of his news listening to NPR. He watches CNN at the gym. He tells me his wife keeps him up to date on the pop culture news, which he would never follow on his own. Like Rita and many others I spoke with, he relies on his friends for updates on the local news. The idea that we are beginning to rely on our own pre-selected communities to keep us informed is almost a throwback to the days before radio. Given our new technologies, the definition of community has changed, which is why we share different information on everything from Yahoo! Answers™ to Facebook to almost anyone's in-box.

Aaron doesn't want news fed to him. He tries to get a sense of whether he trusts the reporter or journalist he's reading or listening to, or whether that person has done his or her homework, as he puts it. He doesn't frequent many blogs; he doesn't have the time to read them and or to make comments. The others I interviewed, working or studying full-time, agree. However, Aaron will click on a link or visit a site if it's one recommended by a friend or if it concerns a topic that interests him.

Some of the Generation Blackberry I spoke with insisted they could find a story's context themselves and didn't need the assistance provided by a reporter, mainstream or otherwise. They didn't seem to think relying on mainstream media analysis would give them a proper perspective. While they acknowledge mainstream journalists might have superior training, they worry that the reporters are under the influence of a chain of command that favors polls and market testing over the pursuit of the truth.

My conversations with these three and with a random sampling of others between eighteen and twenty-nine years of age point to a culture that places great value on the recommendations of friends, who may send them items on a wide array of topics, from critical to silly ("Hey, did you see the story about the guy who saved a grizzly bear from drowning?"). This group (and, with increasing frequency, their parents) are constantly engaged in IMing, texting, and tweeting. It's tempting to assume that Twitter is a fad, used to pass off inane remarks as insightful haikus by celebrities, media people, and politicians who have taken to (or been overtaken by) the power of Twitter. Teenagers haven't rushed to replace their text messages with tweets. Still, Twitter has shown some muscle: during the civil unrest following Iran's elections in the early summer of 2009, tweets were used to report instantly, even as other forms of communication were shut down and reporters were banished or confined to their hotel rooms. Media pundits immediately began theorizing that Twitter represented the new media. Time will tell. Information delivered by tweets is still limited, instantaneous but not always verifiable. But Twitter is a great mechanism for alerting us to news and providing links where we can go for more in-depth stories – if we choose to do the research.

Twitter may turn out to be an ideal medium for a group that seems to wants to know *instantly* what's going on somewhere. The idea that youthful attention can be captured, even for an instant, and asked to follow matters of importance appeals to some people with serious issues on their minds. That's why the Israeli consulate in New York chose to hold an open news conference on Twitter about the battle between Israeli forces and Hamas fighters in Gaza. While some mocked the idea that an official was trying to address a centuries-old conflict within the limitations imposed by tweets, the head of media relations at the consulate was unapologetic. "If someone only speaks Spanish, I speak in Spanish," he said. "If someone is using a platform like Twitter, I want to tweet."[8]

Gore believes in the Internet's possibilities to "foster a cornucopia of points of view and fresh perspectives that force people in rigid frameworks to reassess everything."[9] Gore's Internet is an open marketplace of ideas, one that will create a merit system to allow the best ideas to get the most notice But the Internet's potential, like Twitter, is dependent on the people who use it. I'm less confident than he is that we'll differentiate between "best" and "most popular" or even "most familiar." Maybe I'm still trying to get used to the new type of news editor who has appeared as the antidote to "processed" news – us.

Increasingly, it's citizen bloggers – you and me and anyone else who posts, particularly on news-like sites – who are deciding what constitutes the news. *New York Times* media reporter David Carr illustrated this power shift from traditional news outlets to ordinary citizens by imagining a just-hired reporter in a traditionally busy newsroom who's trying to understand what stories get covered. In Carr's imagination, the wise editor came out of his office to remind the kid, "We decide what the news is."[10]

Carr then pointed out: "That truism still attains; it's just the meaning of the pronoun has changed. Yes, we decide what is news as long as 'we' now includes every sentient human with access to a mouse, a remote, or a cell phone."[11]

This is power: the power to reach hundreds or thousands or millions of readers and influence their perceptions, their opinions, and possibly their actions. Jay Adeson, chief executive for the popular news website *Diggit*, calls it "digital democracy."[12] I belong to and post on a site called *Open Salon*, an online news forum whose tagline is "You Make the Headlines" – and we certainly do. On any given day you can find what appears to be a carefully researched political article featured on the home page along with an article entitled "My Life as a Child Bandit." Popularity combines with the editor picks to determine which stories will get the coveted lead spots and also be noticed on other blogs. Sites like Diggit.com and Reddit.com encourage their subscribers and readers to search the web and alert each other to relevant, interesting, outrageous, and novel stories. Tenacious bloggers can "market" their own posts by sending "shout-outs" to readers through multiple sites, which in turn makes them more popular, which in turn gets them more notice.

What's wrong with allowing the masses – or the portion of the masses that finds the time to blog incessantly – decide what's important, instead of some crusty news editor sequestered in his or her office? Nothing at all, especially if Al Gore's theory about the Internet as a marketplace of ideas kicks in and the most popular blogs also turn out to be the most thoughtful or analytical ones. However, given how hard it is to attract and hold our restless and overwhelmed minds, those ideas have to be presented in a formidable package of crafty graphics, supportive images, heads-up approach, and just the right tone to rise to the top. Conversely, any idea can be presented this way. Sometimes, though, what lies beneath isn't anything to shout about.

The younger set appears to trust the news commentary presented by Jon Stewart on Comedy Central's *The Daily Show*. Many of them seem to feel Stewart is more credible and more willing to tell the truth than broadcast commentators. Stewart, whose onscreen persona mocks the traditional commentators, is the ultimate in cool detachment (Stephen Colbert, another Comedy Central stalwart, plunges so deeply into his right-of-center character that we have to stay on our toes to catch the joke). The knowing irony projected by his commentator and shared with his audience is a large part of his appeal. They know he doesn't *really* believe that either he or the news he's delivering is sacrosanct.

Stewart's lineup of guests is impressive, consisting of heavy-hitters in the literary and political world. He mixes serious questions with silly ones in the manner of an excellent television talk-show host, except he's more provocative and on point than most. While he has always insisted his primary purpose is to entertain, he manages to do so while getting his viewers to listen and think about important issues. Who cares if it's a comedy show?

Stewart has insisted he never intended to pose as or substitute for a trained journalist; his show was designed to make fun of the media's self-importance. Suddenly *he's* the guy everyone trusts to speak the truth. I wonder if that first became clear to him in the fall of 2004, when he appeared on CNN's *Crossfire* to appeal to the show's hosts to forgo theatrical partisanship.

Stewart was doing his usual thing, wrapping a spot-on message inside a comically earnest plea. "Stop hurting America," he implored[13] with a hilariously deadpan delivery. But when co-host Tucker Carlson accused Stewart of going easy on certain *Daily Show* political guests, Stewart was truly incredulous. It's a *comedy* show, he reminded Carlson, adding, "It's interesting to hear you talk about my responsibility...this explains a lot...if the news organizations look to Comedy Central for their cues on integrity."[14] What Stewart was trying to say was that *he* wasn't supposed to be providing balanced commentary or hosting debates; *Crossfire* was, and it was failing miserably. The point was utterly lost on the hosts but not on the viewers or, apparently, on the cable decision-makers who yanked *Crossfire* off the air shortly thereafter.

Poor Jon Stewart. If the *Crossfire* episode was a house falling on Carlson and company, it was the balloon lifting Stewart and his cohorts up, up, and away. Even if he hadn't planned on becoming a trusted source for "straight" political and cultural commentary, he's got the gig. More viewers than ever have decided that someone who seems to know what his job is supposed to be (entertainer) is probably someone more reliable and more credible than someone who's lost his way (presumably others in the news business).

Are we supposed to check the headlines on Google or Yahoo,

but go to Comedy Central for news analysis? Not really, although Al
Gore and Tom Brokaw seem to think this is a splendid idea. The *New
York Times* ran a substantial story in 2008 on Stewart asking, "Is Jon
Stewart the Most Trusted Man in America?"[15] A year later, with the
death of Walter Cronkite, Stewart's name was proposed as a sort of
moral authority replacement. Frankly, anything that gets people talking about serious issues like terror and torture, even if they're laughing
at an Elmo-like puppet named Gitmo, is a step in the right direction.
But let's not anoint Stewart as the steward of the new moral authority,
a title I suspect he'd reject. Thank goodness, because if Jon Stewart is
going to be our source for news, however skewed, he's not going to
automatically get a free pass to the high ground.

More and more, television news remains relevant primarily
when it's irreverent, which may also explain why *Saturday Night
Live* enjoyed some of its best ratings during the 2008 presidential
elections; the impressions by the actors of Sarah Palin, Joe Biden,
and Barack Obama were dead on. At the same time, *YouTube* and
similar Internet venues offer more freedom and the possibility of
a larger audience, which may be why more serious programs are
finding their way online alongside homemade videos showcasing an
assortment of hit-or-miss talents. The traditional televised debates
during that presidential campaign were far less interesting than the
CNN/*YouTube*-sponsored Democratic candidate debate in 2007.
That event, hosted by CNN's Andersen Cooper, somehow felt less
scripted and less restrained, which made it feel more substantive.

Mainstream media – broadcast, cable, and print – hasn't been
able to please too many. It's alternately accused of failing to deliver
in-depth reporting and failing to stay on top of stories brought to life
online. Despite its ownership by apolitical corporations with eyes on
the bottom line, mainstream media is still seen by many Americans
as clearly partisan and liberal in its bias (with the exception of Fox

Television, the *Wall Street Journal,* and a number of talk radio shows).
At the same time, liberals may find media outlets to be increasingly
irresponsible. In an op-ed piece published in the middle of the hotly
contested 2008 primary season, Elizabeth Edwards castigated the
media's attention to fluff over substance. Edwards, the wife of the
two-time candidate and former Senator John Edwards, described
media coverage that spilled ink over silly episodes but provided little
focus on issues of importance to the voters. "Every analysis that is
shortened," she wrote, "every corner that is cut, moves us further
away from the truth until what is left is the Cliffs Notes of the news,
or what I call strobe-light journalism, in which the outlines are accurate enough but we cannot really see the whole picture."[16]

It's both sad and ironic that the affair John Edwards apparently
had during the campaign turned out to be of more interest to the
media and its audience than any articles about Edwards' positions on
labor or healthcare. The story also spotlighted the apparent inability
of mainstream news sources to keep up with breaking news. An
article concerning the affair first surfaced in *The National Enquirer*[17]
and rumors bounced around the Internet with mainstream sources
supposedly unable to verify it. But as David Carr later noted, the
public kept at it; "armed with different standards and megaphones
of their own, nontraditional sources pushed on the story all over the
Web until it finally broke..."[18]

Mere months later, when mainstream media went with stories
about the pregnancy of then-vice-presidential candidate Sarah Palin's
daughter and referenced rumors about whether her mother had faked
her pregnancy, it was castigated for stepping over the line. Readers
didn't come down nearly so hard on the bloggers who circulated the
rumors; at least it appears they kept on reading those blogs.

That last point raises questions concerning Carr's comment
about the public's standards: What exactly *are* those standards? What

do we expect or don't we care about when it comes to picking up news from the web? And when it comes to making our own news, what's acceptable? – surely not posting without checking facts or pushing out unsubstantiated rumors or making assertions or recommendations based on faulty research. We might resent the bias we perceive in how network, cable, and print outlets deliver the news or we may worry about the hidden agendas of their parent companies. But these outlets have a mechanism in place for reviewing and measuring the veracity, fairness, or pertinence of a particular story. What mechanism is operating for the hundreds upon hundreds of blogs and independent news sites? Some work like newspapers, with editors and deputy editors, but many others simply put out unsubstantiated POV stories that look and feel and are presented and promoted as news.

We newly empowered news consumers turned editors who have rejected the moral authority of the "elitist media outlets" have at times been caught up in our own "voice of God" fantasies. It's easy to feel as if we are the new purveyors of truth, especially when receiving rates, tips, kudos, or other gratifying reviews from the readers. Online commenters too often get caught up in the sound of their own voices; they often respond to stories with comments that, as Virginia Heffernan, the *New York Times* media columnist remarked, "are hardly models of astuteness."[19]

Heffernan, in an article called "Comment Is King," used as an example the group of comments made by readers of *Washington Post* and *Slate* magazine columnist Anne Applebaum's articles. She observed that the commenters felt free to criticize, make assumptions, or cast aspersions, but what they "[didn't] do is provide a sustained or inventive analysis of Applebaum's work."[20] Instead they posted illogical arguments or poorly researched rebuttals with the absolute certitude, which "makes it hard to keep listening for the clearer, brighter, rarer voices nearly drowned out in the online din."[21]

For better or for worse, the amateur and semi-professional writer/editors and writer/producers are collectively, if not individually, influencing the cultural and political stories of our time. They potentially reach millions of listeners or viewers, consumers whose brains they're filling up with whatever suits them. Heady stuff. Meanwhile, those readers are texting and twittering they're friends. Some posts gain attention because their true or well written, others because the subject is odd or oddly appealing. The truth of a "factual" presentation becomes beside the point. What we need are collectively acceptable standards that we share with each other and our audiences, particularly for those sites or blogs focused on news stories and important issues.

We readers could stand to be a little more discerning, to listen more carefully to those "brighter, rarer voices" Heffernan mentioned. Fabrice Florin, the founder of *News Trust*, a fact-checking website, suggested that in addition to the proliferation of sites like his, what might be necessary is "news literacy training for the public."[22] That's crucial, as far as I'm concerned. The truth may be out there but it's not necessarily contained within the most popular site or your best friend's email. There's nothing wrong with finding a particular article or blog posting or update to be exciting, entertaining, or even shocking, as long as we remember to ask ourselves: is this true? We can research our way towards an answer but there's an even more basic skill set available to almost any human being who wants to take a step back from the information onslaught. It's called critical thinking.

Chapter Eight

THINKING MADE EASIER

"[People] need to see that being moral is something
more than abstract good-heartedness, that our basic
ways of knowing are inseparable from our basic ways
of being, that how we think and judge in our daily life
reflects who we are..."

Richard Paul—"Ethics Without Indoctrination"

Nearly two years after 9/11, seventy percent of Americans believed Saddam Hussein was involved in planning the attacks
and that at least some of the hijackers were from Iraq.[1] They believed
it in part not simply because they were expressly told it was so, but
because they weren't expressly told it wasn't – at least not until much
later. Believing it was true supported another assumption widely
held by the public at the time: that the United States was justified in
invading Iraq because terrorists from Iraq attacked us on 9/11.

How can anyone disprove something that has lodged in someone else's mind as true? As the scientists I cited in an earlier chapter
pointed out, it's often close to impossible. Convincing our brains
something's not true when we are absolutely convinced it is turns out
to be very hard work. Convincing most people they need to review

their assertions is obviously even harder. They have to feel it's worth the effort it takes to subject any new idea or piece of information to a thorough mental frisking before they let it anywhere near their cerebral cortexes. This is what critical thinking is all about.

My exposure to critical thinking occurred at home; the public school system I attended wasn't designed to deal with overly inquisitive youngsters. In our house, however, we were encouraged to discuss, debate, question, and examine information we heard or read about (even in school!) before settling on certain assumptions we might be inclined to make.

No one has to automatically accept an idea (or an argument, belief, or statement) just because everyone else accepts it. We may come around to fully embracing whatever it is; but first we're going to want to think about it, reflect on it, measure it against what we know, and keep it away from our own preconceived notions and prejudices. This "reflective skepticism" is an important element of critical thinking; it suggests we be hesitant when confronted with those who declare they have the answers.[2]

Most people who haven't been exposed to the term "critical thinking" could be excused for assuming it was about finding fault or focusing on what doesn't work. It's something of a surprise to learn that proponents of critical thinking are just the opposite; they're optimistic idealists who believe that how we think is inseparable from who we are.

All of us think, but our thinking is shaped by preconceptions to which we are introduced in childhood. Assumptions are what we rely on to make sense of the world. Moreover, "The most important decisions we make in our lives...are made on the basis of these assumptions."[3] Nevertheless, assumptions should be readjusted periodically. Why? Think about it this way: if mankind never reexamined and altered widely held assumptions, we might all still believe the world is flat, women aren't capable of holding elected office, and race or ethnicity automatically render certain people superior.

Since some of our collective assumptions *have* changed over time, it's pretty obvious that most of us are engaged in some kind of critical thinking – just not enough. We ought to be subjecting every piece of information we receive (especially the ones with labeled "guaranteed true") to some kind of evaluation process. We won't necessarily reject what we hear once we've given it careful consideration. For example, we may want to take a friend's advice when it comes to his warning that skiing down Dead Man's Pass is dangerous for a novice. But accepting ideas at face value is altogether a different proposition.

There's another good reason to ask questions as often as possible, even of, perhaps especially of, ourselves; and it's biological. According to the current studies of how the brain functions, certainty is not a conscious choice; it's not even a thought process but rather a feeling arising "out of involuntary brain mechanisms that ...function independently of reason."[4] We may feel we know something but that doesn't mean we know it.

Nevertheless, recognizing the limits of our brains, we are fully capable of challenging ourselves and challenging others who claim to be absolutely certain.

Critical thinking has been around for as long as philosophers have thought about what it means to think. Over the last quarter century, there's been more of an effort to move it outside the realm of philosophy and reach a wider audience. Critical thinking books can now be found not only in the philosophy sections of the local library but on bookstore shelves under psychology, self-improvement, business, and even healthcare. The Foundation for Critical Thinking conducts workshops to help teachers equip their students with critical thinking skills as early as the fourth grade. That's a terrific idea; we form many of our assumptions as children. Besides, critical thinking skills could prove invaluable in navigating the hormonal impulses and peer pressures that define adolescence.

Dr. Linda Elder, the Foundation president, and Dr. Richard Paul, who chairs the National Council for Excellence in Critical Thinking, are both educators with decades between them devoted to the subject. Over the past several years, they've ventured jointly and separately into writing books and manuals aimed at a more general audience. Their works have titles such as, *The Art of Asking Essential Questions* and *Taking Charge of the Human Mind.* The dedication to their latest collaboration – a workbook optimistically called *Twenty-Five Days to Better Thinking and Better Living: A Guide for Improving Every Aspect of Your Life* – reads, "To all those who use their thinking to expose hypocrisy and self-deception, and who work to create what is now but a remote dream – a just and humane world."[5]

The workbook is eighty-five easy-to-get-through pages divided into short chapters. Each chapter corresponds to the assigned mental exercise for that day. Reading through the chapter titles might seem like reading a copy of *O* magazine: "Learn to Empathize with Others;" "Be Reasonable;" "Stop Blaming Your Parents;" "Educate Yourself." This is self-improvement at its highest level; and why not?

Elder and Paul deserve kudos for trying to present a complex idea in a simplified form. Certain academic purists might object to these efforts, but I appreciate the help. It's hard enough for me to lasso my mind into some sort of order, let alone train it to improve itself. I'm as wrapped up as the next person in my preconceived notions. How am I supposed to pry my mind open and then train it to remain open? Elder and Paul anticipated my concern: "Welcome to human nature. We are all, to varying degrees, prejudiced. We all stereotype and deceive ourselves. We see ourselves as possessing *the truth.* Yet we all fall prey to human egocentricity – although not to the same degree. None of us will ever be a perfect thinker, but we can all be *better* thinkers."[6]

The authors admitted that some mental strain and discomfort would result from all these exercises. However, if we are willing to address physical fitness with the "no pain, no gain" credo, why not intellectual fitness?

The idea of intellectual fitness is not one that sits well with most Americans. For one thing, the word intellectual gets a bad rap. Many people see it as some sort of process that takes place in a vacuum, or behind the ivy-covered walls of academia. Intellectualism is something associated with hard-to-read books, words with multiple syllables, left-of-center ideas that don't represent American values, and a sort of hoity-toity detachment from the struggles of everyday people living in an everyday world.

As it is, we Americans often feel as if we're constantly lectured about paying more attention to our physical, mental, and financial well-being from endless public and private entities. We understand the consequences of slacking off. In the middle of counting our calories, watching our weight, getting screened for various diseases, keeping up with the latest medical news, keeping up with bills, choosing the right financial plan, or saving enough for retirement, are we now supposed to apply ourselves to learning how to think better?

Yes, we are, because *not* thinking critically also has consequences. We're not all going to reach the highest level of analytical thought, nor are we going to constantly or consciously access our thinking. But when we're information-collecting, in particular when we're doing so in order to make a judgment, a determination, or a choice, we need to approach the information with an open but skeptical mind. I'd venture to say it's not really safe *not* to do so. Just as we must monitor what we eat, and watch what we spend, so we must be aware that the quality of our thinking directly affects the quality of our lives and the lives of those around us.

This may seem obvious, yet the act of thinking critically runs into some stiff resistance from our biases. The way we talk to each other, or *at* or *across* each other, doesn't support a thoughtful approach, either. Our lack of interest in other points of view and our insistence on staying with our position is practically celebrated in what passes for discussion on television, radio, and the Internet. Far too many talk radio shows invite listeners to call in with comments in order, it would seem, to insult them if they don't agree (public radio programming like that found on NPR are notable exceptions in terms of civility). Blogs, as I've pointed out, attract commenters desperate for attention at least as much as information. Rudeness is considered a performance-enhancing method for getting across a point of view.

If American discourse too often teaches us to shut off dissent, it also places much emphasis on statements made with utter certainty, particularly statements that might otherwise be open to discussion. We're so taken with the assurance with which some individuals state their positions, we don't always stop to think about whether what they're saying is true in all circumstances, or even true at all. The people who make such assertions, known as "premature ultimates," are making "statements uttered with such finality and conviction that the possibility of counterarguments is severely reduced."[7] Case closed.

Depending on our point of view, we'll see those who make premature ultimates as take-no-prisoners, stand-up kinds of people or narrow-minded, inflexible types. If we admire the absolute conviction with which the messenger delivers a statement, we might be more willing to accept it as true.

Not every declarative statement is necessarily a premature ultimate, and I don't just mean provable declarations such as "the sun rises in the east." For instance, if society recognizes genocide as immoral, if this is something about which we've reached a point of moral consensus, then to make a statement like "genocide is wrong" isn't to close off argument, because there isn't an argument. We've individually and collectively accepted that genocide is wrong. Even if the governments of countries engaged in acts promoting genocide secretly believe that genocide makes economic or political sense, they wouldn't try to argue that genocide is moral, only that what their government is doing isn't genocide.

When confronted with powerfully presented assertions, most of us are likely to react emotionally before our conscious brain kicks into gear, especially on issues that support our most cherished assumptions. That's what a persuasive speaker tries to do; she appeals to our feelings rather than our intellect. We might not notice our unconscious mind is being summoned. If something excites or outrages us on first hearing or reading, we may go ahead and accept it without being overly concerned whether what we're hearing is absolutely factual.

To give some specific examples: let's say we have a preconceived notion about what it means to be a liberal; we associate the word with higher taxes and questionable values. In that event, we're likely to receive any story or statement using the word liberal with a negative bias. The same holds true if we think of all Southerners as racists, all Republicans as obstructionists, or all Muslims as terrorists. We can say we know better, or that we don't think like that, or even that we don't really hold those kinds of biases. But somewhere behind what Malcolm Gladwell called the locked door of our unconscious mind,[8] our preconceived notions remain strong. We may experience a moment of doubt or a little flash of insecurity; we may wonder whether we might want to reconsider our biases (which we're unlikely to recognize as biases) in the light of new information or in the spirit of tolerance. Yet we can be tipped into accepting a statement in support of our beliefs. By the way, Gladwell's very readable book *Blink* insisted that instincts were real thoughts with a process attached to them. Maybe trusting your gut involves some sort of calculation; but that process is not critical thinking. At most, it's about guessing that something you say or do will produce the best result. That's not enough to change anyone's mindset, least of all our own.

Most of us have emotional reactions; it's part of the glory of being human. We can't count on those reactions for fact-checking, however. I find I have to be very careful to bridge the gap between my often instantaneous emotional reactions to certain kinds of news or information (anger, disbelief, outrage, or joy) and the kind of critical assessment I depend on to sort through what I'm taking in. Emotions have their uses, but they're wildly unpredictable, which makes them less than reliable when processing information. Trusting our emotions or our instincts might well result in a favorable outcome. Nonetheless, we're relying on what *feels* right, not what we *know* is right – and there *is* a difference.

The immediacy of cyberspace communications like email, texts, and tweets can often provoke a quick, unguarded, unconsidered reaction. As a result, the medium is a near-perfect system for not only causing misunderstandings and hurt feelings among friends and colleagues, but also for spreading gossip, innuendo, and outright falsehoods. Here's where instinct doesn't always serve us well.

During the 2008 presidential campaign, a reporter researching an article about voter opinions in Western Pennsylvania came upon a potential voter who told the reporter, "I got an email about Obama refusing to shake hands with the troops in Afghanistan. I don't have time to check to *see if it's true* (italics mine) but it's pretty insulting."[9]

The original email that was circulated was by someone who identified himself as a captain in service; he claimed to have seen Barack Obama "blowing off" troops in Afghanistan. The website Snopes.com extensively researched the account and found that not only was it factually in error, according to an Army spokesperson, but would have been at the very least inappropriate for any Army personnel to have sent out in the first place. In addition, Snopes.com reported receiving a large number of reports from soldiers who had met and even shared a quick meal with Obama. Pictures of the candidate shaking hands with soldiers were then posted online; the originator of the accusatory email then wrote to recant his earlier statements.[10]

I decided to find out if the email received by the discontented Pennsylvanian voter might have been disproved or verified without much difficulty; it could. I spent five or ten minutes online to follow through; I didn't want to rely on my own reaction to the email. Meanwhile, the man quoted above, while declaring he didn't have time to verify the rumor, had already accepted it as true, and had sent it along to friends, relatives, and other acquaintances. Clearly, it made him angry to think Obama might have insulted the men and women fighting in Afghanistan. Likely, he took in the email version of the story (Obama didn't shake hands with the troops), matched it to a preconceived notion about the candidate (Obama doesn't have what it takes to be commander in chief), and came to his conclusion (Obama doesn't support our troops). It would be difficult if not impossible to persuade him that the email information is anything but true. He now *knows* Obama didn't shake hands with the troops.

In the long run, what this one man believed about this one rumor may seem inconsequential. But if a group of people commit to a piece of false or unverifiable information, they may act in a manner that has emotional, economic, political, or social consequences.

The so-called swine flu epidemic in early 2009 didn't originate with pigs, but that didn't stop the Egyptian government from ordering the slaughter of some 400,000 pigs.[11] The act virtually destroyed the livelihoods of Egypt's pig farmers, many of them members of the country's Coptic Christian minority. Some people accused the government of using the threat of an epidemic as an excuse to harass the mostly impoverished farmers. Regardless, the majority Muslim population, disinclined to view favorably anything associated with pork, was probably ready to accept as fact that this particular virus was caused by pigs.

Not all emails, whether about this Democrat, that Republican, this urban legend, or that health advisory, are devised to deliberately trick us into believing falsehoods. These email senders assume they're alerting their friends and acquaintances to a particular set of facts, although they may inadvertently establish or refute the veracity of the information with commentary that reveals their own biases, e.g. "OMG, can you BELIEVE this?" or "How stupid is this?" Then there are those emails, it's fair to assume, that are distributed by people who are counting on our susceptibility to believing as true the first thing we hear, read, or see. One way or the other, we're being manipulated, which should terrify or tick off absolutely everyone. It certainly makes me mad.

What do we do? Let's return to our potential voter residing in an economically depressed area and working hard, the man who didn't check to see whether what he read in an email about candidate Obama was true or not. Let's say he can't find the time to log onto the Internet to do some fact-checking or even write back to the friend or anonymous sender to ask: "How do you know this? Where did you come by this information?" If he even asks himself whether it makes sense that a candidate trying to appeal to a wide variety of voters would be foolish enough to refuse to interact with our troops, then he's taken a step towards critical thinking. There may be plenty of other reasons why our voter in Western Pennsylvania may decide this is not a candidate he can support, but it won't be based on a single incident someone else passed along to him as true. At least I hope not.

I can imagine my friend – the one who said people didn't have time for nuanced thinking – shaking his head as if to remind me that critical thinking isn't something most people are going to be able to manage. Ridiculous, I counter. Reflexive skepticism isn't rocket science. Pausing in the face of new information to perform a mental fact check or ask a question is less about having the time and more about having the inclination.

I suspect if I were to ask a random handful of people, they'd say their thinking was fine and didn't need fine-tuning. We tend to be comfortable relying on long-standing assumptions, especially if we believe we've already thought through a particular issue. Sometimes, however, we continue to absorb only information that supports those assumptions while resisting or rejecting the rest.

That's one big stumbling block when it comes to asking people to engage in critical thinking: we're pretty attached to our biases, habits, feelings, and especially our fears. What is prejudice after all but a preconceived way of judging someone or something? If only we could teach ourselves to respond immediately to our emotional, passionate, and often illogical side of the brain with the admonition to "Calm down. Don't panic. Think a minute. Breathe!" After all, it's something we're taught to do when confronted with immediate danger, although we forget the advice in the heat of the moment, as the near hysteria surrounding healthcare reform continues to demonstrate. But integration was met with similar panic, as hard as it may be to remember. And despite momentary outrage, we now accept that we have to buckle up and that there are places where we can't smoke, two examples of the kind of government "interference" that was formerly seen as intolerable. Gradually, the perceived threat dissipates, even though it seems unforeseeable at the time.

Another problem for critical thinking is that appeals to reason can come across as boring. We've gotten used to verbal brawling, which tends to be dramatic and immediate but doesn't require research, analysis, or deep thought. A whole category of talk radio shows thrive on superficially introducing a topic in order to trade insults with their listeners. Then there are the blog commenters whose need to express themselves quickly and frequently outweighs their interest in reflecting on or assessing the topic at hand.

Thinking critically is both an art and a science. It's something we have to learn and practice until it becomes automatic. But imagine if we could learn to step back from making snap judgments and see if those judgments stand up to scrutiny. Taking time to think through our choices should make us more confident in the choices we make.

Take a minute before you settle down with your old prejudice or the new bit of unverified information you just picked up from your best friend's blog and ask yourself: does this make sense? Am I falling back (or is my friend falling back) on old stereotypes? Can I imagine another way of looking at this issue? Are there other factors to consider here: my experience, the experience of others around me, my needs and also the needs of others? Am I embracing this particular piece of information because it seems fair and it makes sense – or because it confirms my fears or my worst suspicions about something or someone else?

Let's say we accept that critical thinking provides us with the tools to more accurately assess the value of information. Let's say it might even lead us to make better, bias-free, reflective decisions about people or about ideas. Would we still need moral authority to help us find meaning and purpose to our lives?

Chapter Nine

OPEN MIND, OPEN HEART

"The ability to revise beliefs in light of new information is part of what makes having a mind worthwhile."

Austin Dacey—*The Secular Conscience*

The conversation about moral authority in America continues.
We debate our country's ability to be a world leader without it.
We worry the government is poised to assert its moral authority to
make decisions for us. We alternately embrace and reject assumptions about the moral authority of our physicians and we lament the
passing of news commentators whose presumed moral authority
reassured us. In other words, we're all over the map and dangerously
so. We can't seem to get away from the idea that moral authority is
virtuous and a force for good if we just use it the right way. Never
mind that moral authority has been misused and abused for centuries;
we persist in believing we'll be lost without it.

Before he became Pope Benedict XVI, Cardinal Joseph Ratz-
inger attributed the decline of moral authority in the West to our
preference for moral relativism, which he defined as "letting oneself
be tossed and swept along by every wind of teaching." To him, the
decline involved a loss of values and was tied to the absence of

dedication to "a clear faith, based on the Creed of the Church."[1] Presumably, a return to "clear" faith returns us to a moral authority in which the Church defines for us what it is moral to do or believe. Unfortunately, the Church hasn't proven receptive to change and has been slow to respond to sexual improprieties, particularly those that involve children, within its own ranks.

Nevertheless, the cardinal's fears about declining moral authority are shared by a variety of people. Calls for the return of this presumed virtue are found across the theological, political, and social spectrum. Some, like the cardinal, want to return to a traditional authority based on Church doctrine; others describe moral authority in terms of the humanitarian duties of a more activist government. Yet even well-meaning calls for social justice can't redeem moral authority. The notion has become so intertwined with and overtaken by the idea of being certain, or being right, that it's become corrupted.

Those who fret about moral authority's downfall seem to believe that without it we plunge into moral chaos, unable to distinguish right from wrong or good from bad. Theirs is a lowly view of the human race. Then again, given the way people behave towards each other, maybe we really can't trust ourselves to come up with an adequate, let alone inspiring, value system. Look at us – selfish, self-regarding and self-preserving, saddled with faulty brains, ancient prejudices, and primitive inclinations. People aren't to be trusted. Without a definitive someone or something to tell us how to morally pull ourselves up by our bootstraps, we're lost.

I suppose we might view mankind as a step away from reverting to its worst impulses or saddled with original sin; I prefer the idea that human beings are born with "original virtue."[2] We're not simply born free of sin, a blank slate; we're born good, with the capacity to understanding what is right and what is good.

In other words, our conscience – a helpful combination of reason with other psychological impulses such as empathy, compassion, benevolence, and love of others[3] – is our guide. The conscience helps us figure out what makes sense to believe or what seems best to do. Even though we are geared from an evolutionary standpoint towards self-preservation, our conscience turns our attention to the needs of others as well, so that we're as likely as not to act morally.[4]

It's good to imagine our minds and hearts working together instead of constantly fighting with each other for the number-one position, like two children shoving each other out of line. Reason is a conscious process by which we analyze information and weigh consequences; feelings don't seem to operate that way at all. As *Star Trek's* resident Vulcan, Spock, liked to point out, they're illogical. But if our reasoning leads us to question, it's because we desire answers.[5] Desire may not be logical, but it's a great motivator.

With all these tools at our disposal, why not just claim our own moral authority? After all, we're fully equipped to form moral judgments. Yes, we are, but we still have to remember our judgments aren't going to be infallible. There's a limit to what we can *know*. Certainty leads to inflexibility; once we're entrenched, it's difficult to question our own choices. I support Neal Walsch's call to "Listen to your feelings. Listen to your highest thoughts. Listen to your experience;" but I wouldn't advise anyone, as he does: "Whenever any of these differ from what you've been told by your teacher or read in your books, forget the words. Words are the least reliable purveyors of truth."[6]

Blanket statements bother me. Maybe we're not meant to take what Walsch says literally; perhaps he's simply suggesting we don't over-think a particular issue or maybe he's recommending we not believe everything we read. Fine, but why not say that? Why present a false choice between what we read and what we feel? Words are not the enemy of feelings (ask any poet), nor are they *necessarily* unreliable if we know how to think about them. I'm a proponent of listening to the little voice inside me, but I'd like that little voice to be operating with an arsenal of information at its disposal.

One of the paradoxes in living up to our potential as human beings is that we must accept our limits, especially our limits to fully *know*. I've always been amazed by how easily some people come to their conclusions and stick with them even in the face of new information. As I pointed out earlier, modern-day neurologists have discovered that our feeling that we know something is just that – a feeling. We can know we don't like broccoli or are hopeless on rollerblades; but being convinced about something isn't the same as having knowledge of it (remember, people once *knew* the world was flat). Nevertheless, we can't help our feelings of certainty and we sometimes can't help but be drawn to those feelings in others. Certainty feels secure, as if we have our feet on the ground. Notwithstanding how dangerous it can be, how it fuels all sorts of fundamentalist ideas, how it insists on *its* version of the world to the exclusion of other views, we often find certainty is infinitely preferable to the anxiety-producing alternative.

But wait a minute: Even if we acknowledge the difference between *believing* and *knowing*, we still need to make judgments about right and wrong in order to establish our moral baseline. How do we do that without absolute knowledge? We can know what we know, which sounds like advice from a character from *Alice in Wonderland* but simply means: we can know in part. Fallible knowledge allows us to reject moral absolutism, yet still access a set of moral values, since knowing in part "doesn't keep us from thinking that we're right. It just keeps us from thinking that we couldn't possibly be wrong."[7]

The distinction is crucial. Fallibility doesn't negate the moral framework society develops against which we can measure our actions and those of others. But it allows that certain moral "truths" we once held as sacrosanct (women are naturally inferior to men; sex between two partners sharing one gender is immoral) are subject to review.

What about good and evil? We know with absolutely certainty what evil is, don't we? And if we do, can't we also assume that those who commit evil – sociopaths, psychopaths, terrorists – are themselves evil?

No doubt many Americans regarded the attacks on 9/11 as evil. Liberation forces entering German concentration camps during World War II also described what they saw as pure evil, as have those who've witnessed the atrocities committed in Rwanda and Darfur. Certain acts are morally indefensible. Sometimes wrong is just wrong. While I may hesitate to use a word like evil, which has been carelessly misapplied far too often, certain acts may be so heinous, so outside our moral framework that no other word seems nearly strong enough.

If we agree to call certain actions evil, are the perpetrators also evil? Here we run into a problem, in part because we allow so many exceptions. For instance, we're unlikely to see *ourselves* as evil, even if we do something society considers to be evil. We also exempt others, especially when we're trying to balance one bad act against a lifetime of good. Thomas Jefferson owned slaves; in our own times, we view slavery as morally reprehensible, but we don't view Jefferson the man as evil. The loving mother who beats a child to death because she heard God instructing her to exorcize the devil isn't considered evil, but insane. Many such deeds are committed by "people who never made their minds up to be or do evil at all."[8]

The other problem is that calling people evil suggests we know their hearts and minds. When the actor Will Smith suggested Hitler probably *thought* he was doing something good, the critics piled on.[9]

In reality, Smith was astutely noting that identifying the intentions of certain evil-doers requires knowledge we don't have and can't possess.

The truth is, we can't say with absolute certainty that people who commit horrible acts are inherently evil. We can condemn them for their actions; and we can certainly hold them responsible. But we're better off trying to determine which acts are morally defensible and which aren't, instead of trying to determine what those responsible are thinking.

While certainty turns out be of dubious help in making moral determinations, the thought of questioning long-held beliefs throws many people into a state of anxiety. If everything's up for review, aren't we on shaky ground? What does anything mean? Or, what if nothing means anything, in which case, how is it we don't all sink into the abyss?

Here is where our brains perform brilliantly, producing sensations that, while not strictly knowledge, help us to make sense of the world. Other sensations can help us feel a sense of accomplishment or may produce in us strong feelings of faith or spirituality. All these feelings prove our brains are working. They aren't trivial but are "as necessary as hunger and thirst...for survival."[10]

Since we're not likely to focus on brain activity as a means of establishing either our purpose or our value system, we come back to our conscience. What does reason plus empathy allow us to do? For one thing, it might let us might it see not only how things stand but how they could become, which keeps us open to possibilities. Since there's no reason to consider that things might get worse and since most of us are unlikely to expend energy on making things worse, we might find ourselves considering how things might be better and then setting about doing what we need to do to make it happen. That's logical, especially as an alternative to certainty; we don't know what the future will bring but we might as well "...choose the view most likely to improve it."[11]

If we decide that we humans are potentially good people, then we can choose on our own to be moral people without being told. Not that the religious kind of faith can't persuade us to be good (it can), but our decision to be good can't rely on rewards, punishments, commandments, or instructions. Whatever our religion, whoever our God, it's our conscience that must dictate our choices. We may believe it to be divinely inspired or the result of inspired evolution. Either way, the conscience is capable of developing, offering, and revising its own moral language. We have free will and we have the freedom to choose.

We have so much going for us: the ability to reason and the opportunity to pair our powers of reason with empathy, desire, and the possibility that all might turn out for the best. What gets in the way?

Fear, for one thing. As Al Gore succinctly observed: "The relationship between faith, reason, and fear sometimes resembles the children's game of rock, paper, scissors. Fear displaces reason, reason challenges faith, faith overcomes fear...Fear, however, can disrupt the easy balance between reason and faith – especially irrational fear of a kind less readily dispelled by reason."[12]

Gore is being polite; fear can trample reason and grind it to dust. He also noted that fear makes us yearn for the consolation found in certainty. "Both religious faith and uncomplicated explanations of the world are even more highly valued at a time of great fear."[13] Gore isn't slamming religion but is instead criticizing an interpretation of faith that contradicts reason. Faith is not the enemy of reason; fear is, something we seem to forget when we're afraid and searching for answers.

Most of us have, and need to have, the instincts to react in a dangerous situation. Burton called these "no-thought-necessary reflexive reaction[s]."[14] We'll react to the snarling dog, the oncoming train, or the man yelling obscenities in public. Fear produces the adrenaline rush we need to run as fast as our legs can carry us, even if it's towards the threat, in order to save a child from the dog, the train, or the man with the knife. Since children often don't have those instincts, we may try to instill in them a sense of caution ("Hot!" "Watch out!" Be careful!") by underscoring our admonitions with a sense of urgency. We don't want little Johnny to burn his hand or fall down the stairs or poke his eye with a fork. But we also don't need or want him to grow up fearing fire, avoiding the stairs or eating with his hands.

While reacting to imminent danger may preclude reasoning (there's nothing logical about rushing into traffic to save your child and there doesn't need to be), fear becomes more complicated, and more dangerous, when it activates our prejudices. Fear is often linked with ignorance to describe bias, but that isn't a complete explanation. Sometimes we lack information; oftentimes we have it, but don't use it. Reason is deliberate, whereas fear swamps us with a rush of physical sensations that keep us from thinking clearly, never mind critically. This is precisely what makes fear-based proselytizing, whether spiritual or political, so successful. The message doesn't ask us to consider, but instead demands that we be afraid.

What does fear have to do with moral decision-making? Consider this: To be truly ethical, we must be able to access "an impartial but still impassioned moral point of view that's not just about [us] but also about others."[15] But fear doesn't recognize impartiality. Fear is about identifying a threat. The threat may be eternal damnation for those who do not follow a certain set of rules. Or it could take the form of "others" who might steal our jobs, overburden our services, menace our way of life, or harm our families. The most disturbing aspect of the post-9/11 response was not that terrorists or anthrax-wielding crazies were willing to kill us. It was how easily we acquiesced to a message of fear so potent that to question the message was to bring cries of treason from our fellow citizens.

Fear is a moral and spiritual dead-end that invokes the worst in us. Fear manages to poison our thoughts, narrow our vision, and close off our options. Moreover, fear, when it relates to a perceived threat and not a tangible, imminent one, is inherently unreasonable. That hasn't stopped me from feeling afraid of the unknown – the potential of crippling disease, the possibility of loneliness, the intentions of people who seem bent on my destruction, or the fate of the planet. Sometimes reason reminds me I have a choice about whether or not I want to dwell on what I don't know with any certainty. Sometimes it doesn't.

It's not easy to step back from fear, especially when there are so many more issues that appear to divide us than to unite us. Even if we manage to quell the terror that strikes whenever we worry about losing our jobs, managing our health, going through another attack, growing old or not growing old – even if we could manage to lift our heads up from the concerns that overwhelm us – what would we see but poverty and war, rape and genocide, hunger and anger, and a planet whose resources are being depleted? Where can reason take us then? Here too, we have a choice, if we can keep not only an open mind but an open heart. We can choose hope.

Chapter Ten

HOPE IS A FOUR-LETTER WORD

"Sanity may be madness but the maddest of all is to see
life as it is and not as it should be"

Don Quixote

"If life is to be sustained hope must remain, even where
confidence is wounded, trust impaired."

Erik Erikson

The pursuit of hope looks good on paper. As a way of conducting our lives, however, hope might seem inaccessible, or at the very least naïve. In dealing with our daily lives or becoming aware of how many people in the rest of the world struggle just to get by, we can't help but wonder: how reasonable is hope?

Just as we might, at one time or another, need to write out lists of work or life goals, we can make a mental list of things about which to be positive. For example, we can look at how far we've come as a species, as Susan Neiman suggests.[1] No, advances haven't taken place in all parts of the world; our access to information means we're more aware than ever that inequality and injustice persist and that humans are still sold into slavery, butchered, imprisoned, or tortured.

But if we go back in time and see what we *have* accomplished, we can look forward to what more we might accomplish.

We can also look to enduring human conditions. Jane Goodall, best known for her studies of indigenous chimpanzee populations, listed her reasons to hope as: "the [existence of] the human brain; the resilience of nature; the energy and enthusiasm that is found... among young people; [and] the indomitable human spirit."[2]

Hope can't eradicate uncertainty; reason doesn't allow us to know it all. And living with uncertainty requires a kind of letting go, which presents most of us with a big learning curve. As we've seen, shaking people loose from their comfortable and familiar assumptions is daunting. Then again, as anyone who has gone through a life-changing experience will admit, sometimes life itself shakes us loose whether we're ready or not. Not long after her own journey of self-discovery, Elizabeth Gilbert (who wrote the popular *Eat, Pray, and Love*) noted: "Sometimes it seems like the only job of the world is to gently (and not so gently) separate us from our deepest assurances, exposing us once again to that ultimate moral teaching tool: humility."[3]

Uncertainty can apparently cause contentment. Dr. Burton waxed poetic about the joy of coming to terms with uncertainty, describing it as "[t]he sense of an inner quiet born of acknowledging my limitations..."[4] In fact, one of the most beautiful arguments in favor of uncertainty was written by the novelist Anne Perry: "To know everything [is] to destroy the infinite possibilities of...hope."[5]

Embracing uncertainty and choosing to hope may be every bit as liberating as these writers and others make it out to be; yet it's harder than it sounds. Before 9/11, I assumed I'd accepted uncertainty and maybe even humility. I'd already acknowledged I couldn't fully understand the complex nature of the universe or the meaning of our existence. When Jim was killed, I didn't ask, "Why me?" or struggle to come to terms with what the fates has sent me. I didn't seek solace in comfortable assumptions or become furious those assumptions had been shaken. I didn't assign blame or look for resolution.

Still, no amount of critical thinking could have prepared me for level of anguish and anxiety I felt following my husband's death in such a public and violent manner. For a long time, I felt completely unmoored, uncertain even about even my own survival. Most of the images in my mind from that period invoke an endless sea, a vast expanse of unoccupied horizon, and a rudderless boat with me in it. I felt not only devastated but also helpless; not only helpless but hopeless. I didn't seem to know what to do, even as I set about trying to do something, anything – advocate, write, reconnect with old friends, make new ones, or open up to all those possibilities I'd read about. I couldn't see where they were. I struggled to find purpose and meaning. I accepted uncertainty without fear but also sadly, without hope.

No one person, no single experience, no specified passage of time has led me to the gradual discovery of hope. Yet it now seems perfectly logical, perfectly reasonable to hope for the best. Some days I feel as if I'm still adrift, but other days I feel as if I'm on course. On those days, I think, *Who knows?* and feel curiously contented not to have an answer.

My problem with moral authority is that the hope it promises is false, lacking in opportunity or possibility. Moral authority is far too reliant on a fixed set of assumptions. "This is how things are," it says. "I am right; we are right – no need to discuss anything further." Moral authority is anathema to thinking, questioning, examining, reasoning, or wondering – the talents with which we humans have been gifted and which we Americans in particular are fortunate to be able to freely employ. The whole notion of moral authority contradicts everything we know about how our brains work, how our consciences should work, and maybe even how our souls might work.

Uncertainty, on the other hand, presents all sorts of possibilities: what about, what if, why not? We could fear uncertainty, but I'd much rather we all accepted it or, better yet, embraced it. After all, what we don't know absolutely is what we can imagine, invent, dream, or dare to hope.

ACKNOWLEDGEMENTS

I 've had much-appreciated assistance from several friends and acquaintances, including:

Leif Haase, who believed in this book from the beginning and whose rigorous intellectualism guided me through the difficult process of starting this project. That he managed to find time for me while juggling a cross-country move, a new job, a new baby daughter, and work on his own book was nothing short of remarkable;

Peter Trachtenberg, an impressively erudite and experienced writer, who challenged me to prove my points, disagreed agreeably, and provided much-needed encouragement;

Peter Meyer, a writer and editor whose insights into and contacts in the world of publishing proved to be both helpful and illuminating;

David Hingston, who brought a personal and intelligent "everyman" perspective to his assessments;

Marly Cornell, my editor, whose expertise, grace, and good humor was invaluable to the process and has yielded both a friend and future collaborator;

My **loyal band of friends and blog readers**, who have provided me with more purpose and structure than they can imagine;

Deborah Stern, sister, friend, thoughtful reader, and all-around smart person who had significant input into virtually every phase of this journey, from concept to completion and beyond. Her help in getting me to stick to the point was invaluable, especially because she believed I had a point worth making. Anyone and everyone who wants to write a book, particularly one on a little-discussed and widely misunderstood topic, should have at least one friend like that.

ABOUT THE AUTHOR

Nikki Stern worked as a public relations executive before the death of her husband in the World Trade Center on 9/11. While serving on the board and as the first executive director of Families of September 11, a national organization for families affected by the terrorist attacks, she was co-recipient of a Common Ground Award in 2005 from the global conflict transformation group, Search for Common Ground. She has maintained advocacy roles on the advisory boards of Project Rebirth, Americans for Informed Democracy, and the Public Diplomacy Collaborative at Harvard University's Ash Institute for Democratic Governance and Innovation. Her writing has appeared in the *New York Times*, *Newsweek*, and *USA Today*.

Nikki retains an interest in public engagement and global diplomacy as well as topics concerning women, writing, and humor. She blogs regularly about politics, culture, entertainment, and other issues of both greater and lesser importance at www.1womansvu.com.

Notes

Chapter 1

1. "Moral Authority," Wiktionary 18 January 2008, (accessed 11 February 2008) http://en.wiktionary.org/wiki/moral_authority.

2. "authority," Merriam-Webster Online Dictionary 2009, (accessed 11 February 2008) http://www.merriam-webster.com/dictionary/authority.

3. "moral," Merriam-Webster Online Dictionary 2009, (accessed 11 February 2008) http://www.merriam-webster.com/dictionary/moral.

4. Bernard Gert, "The Definition of Morality," Stanford Encyclopedia of Philosophy, (accessed 11 February 2008) http://plato.stanford.edu/entries/morality-definition/.

5. Steven Pinker, "The Moral Instinct," New York Times Magazine 13 January 2008, (accessed 11 February, 2008) http://www.nytimes.com/2008/01/13/magazine/13Psychology-t.html.

6. Cass Sunstein, Going to Extremes: How Like Minds Unite and Divide (New York, NY: Oxford University Press, 2009) 2.

7. Sam Wang and Sandra Aamodt, "Your Brain Lies to You," New York Times 27 June 2008, (accessed 6 July 2008) http://www.nytimes.com/2008/06/27/opinion/27aamodt.html.

8. Man of the Year, dir. Barry Levinson, perf. Robin Williams, Universal, 2006. (accessed 28 June 2008) http://www.imdb.com/title/tt0483726/quotes.

9. Susan Jacoby, The Age of American Unreason (New York, NY: Pantheon Books, 2008) 211.

10. Jacoby xx.

11. "Pessimistic U.S.," Huffington Post 20 May 2007, (accessed 9 April 2009) http://www.huffingtonpost.com/huff-wires/20070520/pessimistic-us/.

12. "Outlook on Economy Is Brightening, New Poll Finds," The New York Times 7 April 2009, (accessed 9 April 2009) http://www.nytimes.com/2009/04/07/us/politics/07poll.html?_r=1&hp.

13. Neale Donald Walsch (accessed 5 October 2008) http://www.nealedonaldwalsch.com/.

Chapter 2

1. "Nous Sommes Tous Americans," Le Monde 13 September 2001, (accessed 8 August 2008) http://www.lemonde.fr/opinions/article/2007/05/23/nous-sommes-tous-americains_913706_3232.html.

2. Nikki Stern, "Our Grief Doesn't Make Us Experts," Newsweek 13 March 2006, (accessed 8 August 2008) http://www.newsweek.com/id/46878.

3. Dorothy Rabinowitz, "The 9/11 Widows: Americans Are Beginning to Tire of Them," The Wall Street Journal 14 April 2004, (accessed 8 August 2008) http://www.opinionjournal.com/medialog/?id=110004950.

4. CNN coverage of Cindy Sheehan protest, aired August 25, 2005. Transcripts (accessed 9 August 2008) at http://transcripts.cnn.com/TRANSCRIPTS/0508/21/rs.01.html.

5. Maureen Dowd, "Why No Tea and Sympathy?," New York Times 10 August 2005, (accessed 8 August 2008).

6. Christopher Hitchens, "Cindy Sheehan's Sinister Piffle," Slate Magazine 15 August 2005, (accessed 8 August 2008) http://www.slate.com/id/2124500/.

7. Wayne Jackson, "The Value of Human Suffering," The Christian Courier 15 February 1999, (accessed 8 August 2008) http://www.christiancourier.com/articles/52-the-value-of-human-suffering.

8. Neal Gabler, "Toward a New Definition of Celebrity," Norman Lear Center Magazine 2001, (accessed 9 August 2008) http://www.learcenter.org/pdf/Gabler.pdf.

Chapter 3

1. "U.S. Religious Landscape Survey," Pew Forum on Religion and Public Life 2008, (accessed 6 March 2008) http://religions.pewforum.org/reports.

2. David Van Biema, "Behind America's Different Perceptions of God," Time Magazine 23 October 2006, (accessed 6 March 2008) http://www.time.com/time/nation/article/0,8599,1549413,00.html.

3. David Sipress, Cartoon #124965, The New Yorker, 10 March 2008, (accessed 6 March 2008) http://www.newyorker.com/magazine/toc/2008/03/10/toc_20080303.

4. Pew Forum on Religious and Public Life, http://religions.pewforum.org/reports#.

5. Ben Stein, "Who are Nick and Jessica?" CBS Sunday Morning 18 December 2005, (accessed 7 March 2008) http://www.cbsnews.com/video/watch/?id=1134772n%3fsource=search_video.

6. "Text of Romney 'Faith in America' Speech," WCVB-TV Boston, MA 6 December 2007 (accessed 9 March 2008) http://www.thebostonchannel.com/politics/14789305/detail.html.

7. Austin Dacey, The Secular Conscience (Amherst, NY: Prometheus Books, 2008) 51.

8. "Text of John F. Kennedy's Speech to the Greater Houston Ministerial Association," The American Presidency Project 12 September 1960, (accessed 7 March 2008) http://www.presidency.ucsb.edu/ws/index.php?pid=25773.

9. Nicholas D. Kristoff, "Evangelicals a Liberal Can Love," New York Times 3 February 2008, (accessed 13 March 2008) http://www.nytimes.com/2008/02/03/opinion/03kristof.html.

10. Theodore Bikel, "Faith, Politics and the Good Deed Factor," New York Times 4 February 2008, (accessed 13 March 2008) http://www.nytimes.com/2008/02/06/opinion/l06kristof.html.

11. Lewis Black, (accessed 8 May 2008) http://www.lewisblack.com/me_of_little_faith.ASP.

12. Christopher Hitchens, God Is Not Great: How Religion Poisons Everything (New York, NY: Hachett Book Company, 2007) 5-6.

13. Madeline Albright, The Mighty and the Almighty: Reflections on America, God and World Affairs (New York, NY: Harper Perennial Books, 2006) 23.

Chapter 4

1. William J Bennett, Why We Fight: Moral Clarity and the War on Terrorism (New York, NY: Doubleday Books, 2003) 16.

2. Bennett 17.

3. Bennett 55.

4. Bennett 145.

5. Ward Churchill, On the Justice of Roosting Chickens: Reflections on the Consequences of U.S. Imperial Arrogance and Criminality (London, UK: AK Press, 2003) 19.

6. Partial transcript of comments from the September 13, 2001 telecast of the 700 Club (accessed 20 April, 2009) http://www.actupny.org/YELL/falwell.html.

7. Bennett 153.

8. Andrew Kohut and Bruce Stokes, America Against the World: How We Are Different and Why We Are Disliked (New York, NY: Times Books, Henry Holt and Company, 2006) 100.

9. Madeline Albright, The Mighty and the Almighty: Reflections on America, God and World Affairs (New York, NY: Harper Perennial Books, 2006) 52, 53.

10. Albright 57.

11. Albright 161.

12. Kohut and Stokes 76.

13. Albright 32.

14. Reported by BBC News, October 7, 2005, (accessed 11 May, 2009) http://news.bbc.co.uk/2/hi/americas/4320586.stm; see also "Israel and the Arabs, Elusive Peace" http://news.bbc.co.uk/1/hi/programmes/elusive_peace/.

15. Kohut and Stokes 9.

16. Kohut and Stokes 47.

17. Daniel Johnson, "America's Moral Authority," New York Sun 1 May 2008, (accessed 20 May 2009) http://www.nysun.com/opinion/amsericas-moral-authority/7681/.

18. Albright 158.

19. Ron Suskind, The Way of the World: A Story of Truth and Hope in an Age of Extremism (New York, NY: Harper Collins, 2008) 14.

20. Ron Suskind on "The Daily Show," 11 August 2008, (accessed 20 May, 2009) http://www.

thedailyshow.com/video/index.jhtml?videoId=178985&title=ron-suskind.

21. DC Rapier, "The Myth of American Moral Authority," Op-Ed News 16 August 2008, (accessed 18 May 2009) http://www.opednews.com/articles/The-Myth-of-American-Moral-by-DC-Rapier-080816-781.html.

22. DC Rapier.

23. Suskind 395.

Chapter 5

1. Gabler http://www.learcenter.org/pdf/Gabler.pdf.

2. Andrew Johnson and Andy McSmith, "Children Say Being Famous is the Best Thing in World," The Independent (UK) 18 December 2006, (accessed 4 Nov. 2008) http://www.independent.co.uk/news/uk/this-britain/children-say-being-famous-is-best-thing-in-world-429000.html.

3. Scott Sonner, "Haysbert: Prez role on '24' may have helped Obama," USA Today 2 July 2008, (accessed 4 November 2008) http://www.usatoday.com/life/people/2008-07-01-haysbert-obama_N.htm.

4. Lawrence O'Donnell, Jr., "Where Are You, Dream Candidate?" Washington Post 20 May 2007, (accessed 4 November 2008) http://www.washingtonpost.com/wp-dyn/content/article/2007/05/18/AR2007051801648_2.html.

5. Frank Rich, "Wall-E for President," New York Times 6 July 2008, (accessed 4 November 2008) http://www.nytimes.com/2008/07/06/opinion/06rich.html.

6. Theodore Dalyrimple, "Guided by the Stars," Los Angeles Times 20 May 2007, (accessed 10 November 2008) http://articles.latimes.com/2007/may/20/opinion/op-dalrymple20.

7. Josh Tyrangiel, "Bono's Mission" Time Magazine 4 Mar. 2002, (accessed10 November 2008) http://www.time.com/time/covers/1101020304/story.html.

8. Dalyrimple http://articles.latimes.com/2007/may/20/opinion/op-dalrymple20.

9. Jeffrey M. Jones, "Hillary Edges Out Oprah as Most Admired Woman in '07," Gallup 26 December 2007, (accessed10 November 2008) http://www.gallup.com/poll/103462/hillary-edges-oprah-most-admired-woman-07.aspx.

10. "Commentators Talk More On the 'Oprah' Effect," Tell Me More, NPR 30 November 2007, (accessed14 November 2008) http://www.npr.org/templates/story/story.php?storyId=16765636.

11. Ann Oldenburg, "The Divine Miss Winfrey?" USA Today 11 May 2006, (accessed14 November 2008) http://www.usatoday.com/life/people/2006-05-10-oprah_x.htm.

12. Martin Bertello, "Is Oprah the most dangerous woman in the world? Internet evangelist, Bill Keller says 'Yes!'" WDC Media 3 March 2008, (accessed15 November 2008) http://www.wdcmedia.com/newsArticle.php?ID=3863.

13. Ray Richmond, "Oprah's Big Give" The Hollywood Reporter 28 February 2008, (accessed15 November 2008) http://www.hollywoodreporter.com/hr/television/reviews/article_display.jsp?&rid=10733.

14. Peter Birkenhead, "Oprah's Ugly Secret," Salon.com 5 March 2007, (accessed 15 November 2008) http://www.salon.com/mwt/feature/2007/03/05/the_secret/.

Chapter 6

1. Jonathon Imber, Trusting Doctors: The Decline of Moral Authority in American Medicine (Princeton, NJ: Princeton University Press, 2008) 12.

2. Imber 169.

3. John D. Lantos, MD, Do We Still Need Doctors? (New York, NY: Routledge, 1997) 164.

4. Tara Parker-Pope, "Doctor and Patient, Now At Odds," New York Times 29 July 2008, (accessed 18 November 2008) http://query.nytimes.com/gst/fullpage.html?res=9B07E5D8133 AF93AA15754C0A96E9C8B63.

5. Parker-Pope http://query.nytimes.com/gst/fullpage.html?res=9B07E5D8133AF93AA15754 C0A96E9C8B63.

6. Parker-Pope http://query.nytimes.com/gst/fullpage.html?res=9B07E5D8133AF93AA15754 C0A96E9C8B63.

7. Lantos 159.

8. Jim Rutenberg and Jackie Calmes, "False 'Death Panel' Rumor Has Some Familiar Roots," New York Times 14 August, 2009 (accessed 1 September, 2009) http://www.nytimes. com/2009/08/14/health/policy/14panel.html.

9. Kirk Johnson, "Montana Court Rule on Assisted Suicide," New York Times 1 September 2009 (accessed 1 September 2009) http://www.nytimes.com/2009/09/01/us/01montana. html?_r=1&hp.

10. "Survey: Many Believe in Divine Intervention," CNN 18 August 2008, (accessed18 November 2008) http://www.hods.org/pdf/press/cnn.pdf.

11. Lantos 70.

12. Sheri Fink, "Strained by Katrina, A Hospital Faced Deadly Choices," New York Times 25 August, 2009 (accessed 1 September 2009) http://www.nytimes.com/2009/08/30/ magazine/30doctors.html?pagewanted=1&_r=1&ref=magazine.

13. Lantos 6.

14. Kevin Sack, "Doctors Say 'I'm Sorry' Before 'See You in Court'," New York Times 18 May 2008, (accessed 19 May 2008) http://www.nytimes.com/2008/05/18/us/18apology.html.

Chapter 7

1. Kurt Andersen, "Meet the Press Now" New York Magazine 10 July 2008, (accessed 2 April 2009) http://nymag.com/news/imperialcity/48510/.

2. "Public Attitudes," Pew Project for Excellence in Journalism Apr. 2006, (accessed 5 April 2009) http://www.stateofthenewsmedia.com/2006/narrative_overview_publicattitudes. asp?cat=8&media=1.

3. Pew Project for Excellence in Journalism http://www.stateofthenewsmedia.com/2006/

narrative_overview_publicattitudes.asp?cat=8&media=1.

4. Matthew Gentzkow and Jesse M. Shapiro, "Media Bias and Reputation," Journal of Political Economy 2 April 2006, (accessed 5 April 2009) http://www.nber.org/papers/w11664.

5. Lewis H. Lapham, Gag Rule: On the Suppression of Dissent and the Stifling of Democracy (New York, NY: The Penguin Press, 2004) 91.

6. Al Gore, The Assault on Reason (New York, NY: Penguin Books, 2007) 6.

7. Noam Cohen, "The Toughest Q's Answered in the Briefest Tweets," New York Times 3 January 2009, (accessed 14 April 2009) http://www.nytimes.com/2009/01/04/weekinreview/04cohen.html.

8. Gore 262.

9. Gore 265.

10. David Carr, "All of Us, the Arbiters of News," New York Times 10 August 2008, (accessed 14 April 2009) http://www.nytimes.com/2008/08/11/business/media/11carr.html.

11. Carr http://www.nytimes.com/2008/08/11/business/media/11carr.html.

12. Noam Cohen, "Spinning a Web of Lies at Digital Speed," New York Times 12 Oct. 2008, (accessed 14 April 2009) http://www.nytimes.com/2008/10/13/business/media/13link.html.

13. "Jon Stewart on 'Crossfire'" 15 Oct. 2004, (accessed 4 December 2008) http://www.youtube.com/watch?v=vmj6JADOZ-8.

14. Jon Stewart http://www.youtube.com/watch?v=vmj6JADOZ-8.

15. Michiko Kakutani, "Is Jon Stewart the Most Trusted Man in America?" New York Times 15 August 2008, (accessed 4 December 2008) http://www.nytimes.com/2008/08/17/arts/television/17kaku.html.

16. Elizabeth Edwards, "Bowling 1, Health Care 0," New York Times, 27 April 2008, (accessed 4 December 2008) http://www.nytimes.com/2008/04/27/opinion/27edwards.html#.

17. Mike Walker, "Presidential Cheating Scandal! Alleged Affair Could Wreck John Edwards' Campaign Bid," The National Enquirer 10 October 2007, (accessed 4 December 2008) http://www.nationalenquirer.com/john_edwards_cheating_scandal/celebrity/64271.

18. Carr http://www.nytimes.com/2008/08/11/business/media/11carr.html.

19. Virginia Heffernan, "Comment Is King," New York Times 23 April 2009, (accessed 28 April 2009) http://www.nytimes.com/2009/04/26/magazine/26wwln-medium-t.html.

20. Heffernan http://www.nytimes.com/2009/04/26/magazine/26wwln-medium-t.html.

21. Heffernan http://www.nytimes.com/2009/04/26/magazine/26wwln-medium-t.html.

22. Cohen http://www.nytimes.com/2008/10/13/business/media/13link.html.

Chapter 8

1. Dana Milbank and Claudia Deane, "Hussein Link to 9/11 Lingers in Many Minds," The Washington Post 6 September 2003, (accessed 11 January 2009) http://www.washingtonpost. com/ac2/wp-dyn/A32862-2003Sep5?language=printer.

2. Brookfield 9.

3. Brookfield 45.

4. Robert A. Burton, M.D., On Being Certain: Believing You Are Right Even When You're Not (New York, NY: St. Martin's Press, 2008) xi.

5. Linda Elder and Richard Paul, Twenty-Five Days to Better Thinking and Better Living: A Guide for Improving Every Aspect of Your Life (New York, NY: Prentice-Hall, 2006) xiv.

6. Elder and Paul xxi.

7. Brookfield 46.

8. Malcolm Gladwell, Blink (New York, NY: Little Brown, 2005) 49-71.

9. Michael Powell, "Rural Swath of Big State Tests Obama," New York Times 21 Aug. 2008, (accessed 12 January 2009) http://www.nytimes.com/2008/08/21/us/politics/21penn.html.

10. "Barack Obama in Afghanistan," Snopes.com 26, July 2008, (accessed 12 January 2009) http://www.snopes.com/politics/obama/afghanistan.asp.

11. Phillipe Naughton, "Egyptian Christians Riot After Swine Flu Cull," The Times of London, 29April 2009, (accessed 2 May 2009) http://www.timesonline.co.uk/tol/news/world/africa/article6193785.ece.

Chapter 9

1. Austin Dacey, The Secular Conscience (Amherst, NY: Prometheus Books, 2008) 9.

2. "Original Virtue" The Jewish Encyclopedia (accessed 21 January, 2009) http://www.jewishencyclopedia.com/view.jsp?artid=86&letter=V. The term was coined by S. Levy to contrast to the idea of "original sin." It identifies the specifically Jewish concept that God visits the virtues of the fathers upon the children for His name's sake and as a mark of grace, providing the children continue the piety of their parents.

3. Dacey 18.

4. Dacey 120,121.

5. Neiman 185.

6. Walsch.

7. Dacey 135.

8. Neiman 331.

9. Karin, Salkin "Will Smith Explains Hitler Quote," People Magazine 26 December 2007, (accessed 7 January 2009) http://www.people.com/people/article/0,20168278,00.html.

10. Burton 177, 180-183.

11. Neiman 192.

12. Gore 45.

13. Gore 55.

14. Burton 108.

15. Dacey 177.

Chapter 10

1. Neiman 282.

2. Jane Goodall, Reason for Hope: A Spiritual Journey (New York, NY: Grand Central Publishing, 2000) 233.

3. Elizabeth Gilbert, "Certainty," O: The Oprah Magazine (November 2008) 233.

4. Burton xii.

5. Anne Perry, Buckingham Palace Gardens (New York, NY: Ballantine Books, 2008) 115.

INDEX

public's standards, 100–101

younger generation's sources, 92–95

News Trust, 102

newspapers. *See* news media

Newsweek, op-ed piece about reverence for 9/11 families, 21–22

9/11 activists, 22

9/11 attacks

brought on ourselves, 47

response to, 45–46

retaliation, 46

9/11 families

backlash in media, 23

moral authority of, 21–23

point of view, 20, 22

public need to know about, 19–20, 28

reverence shown to, 21–22

Nye, Joseph, 52–53

O

Obama, Barack, 38–39, 65–66, 110–111

Op-Ed News, 54

O'Reilly, Bill, 48

The O'Reilly Factor, 86–87

original virtue, 116

P

Palin, Sarah, 39, 100

Parker-Pope, Tara, 74

patients' rights, 77

patriotism, 48, 51

Paul, Richard, 106–107

S

Winfrey, Oprah, 64–69
world domination, 51
World Trade Center site as sacred ground, 31–32

Y

YouTube, 99